# WIN-WIN PRESENTATIONS

John Spencer

TO ALBERT — YOU DON'T NEED THIS BOOK! I KNOW YOU LOVE BEING IN FRONT OF AN AUDIENCE AND DO A WONDERFUL JOB OF IT.

CHEERS

# Win-Win Presentations™

*How To Deliver Winning*

*Presentations with Confidence*

## *Dedication*

I would like to dedicate this book to my family. My wife Gaye for being the wind under my wings. My son Ted and his wife Elaine for being so positive and enthusiastic. My son Scott for his sense of adventure and inspiring me with his incredible writing talents. And my grandchildren Annabelle and Justin ... because they bring such joy to the world.

## AKNOWLEDGEMENTS

Without the insights garnered from A) running seminars on presentation techniques and seeing thousands of people tackle the ultimate challenge of improving their presentations and B) conducting countless presentations to audiences around the world this book would not have been written. They proved to me that anyone can learn new skills and techniques that instantly improve presentations, impress an audience, and enhance confidence. In other words, a win-win!

*Thanks to all of them for*

*inspiring me and teaching*

*me so well.*

# Table of Contents

Introduction

Chapter 1 – Replacing Stress With Confidence

Chapter 2 – Your Audience Craves Confidence

Chapter 3 – Fake It 'Til You Make It

Chapter 4 – Your Roadmap To Success

Chapter 5 – Visualize It!

Chapter 6 – Don't Sweat The Distracting Stuff

Chapter 7 – Selling Your Ideas

Chapter 8 – Crossing The Virtual Divide

Chapter 9 – The Checkout List

# WIN-WIN PRESENTATIONS

*Presenting Confidently To Reach Mutual Goals*

## Introduction

Yes you can! Yes, you can learn how to successfully present your ideas naturally and "be yourself" so that your audience and you leave happy. This is all about **replacing stress with confidence.**

This book is for anyone who wants to create truly outstanding presentations so that you and your audience have a win-win experience.

Win-win presentations are similar to win-win negotiations where both parties (in this case the presenter and audience members) walk away having achieved their goals. In fact, a presentation that leaves both parties feeling like winners.

I can assure you that the tips and techniques in this book will help you to build on your own capabilities and provide you with the insights and key ideas to develop and deliver first-class presentations. If that's what you want to do... then you have come to the right place. Learn what it takes to do a topnotch job of conducting a presentation with confidence and panache.

Oh, and by the way, if you're like millions of other people, you're well aware that the very act of having the spotlight turn on you and giving a virtual or in-person presentation is one of the most stressful activities that you can engage in. This book will help you to tackle the fear factor related to giving presentations head-on.

Please remember one thing. Up to this point in your life you've been able to handle every single challenge that has come your way. And so, my friend, be assured that you will not only "get through" your next presentation but will excel at it!

Yes, I don't want you to just survive your next presentation (and you will), I want to show you how you can master the art of presenting and turn your very next presentation into one of the most enjoyable, fulfilling, and stress-free experiences you can imagine!

Here's what we'll be covering in this book:

# CHAPTER 1

# REPLACING STRESS WITH CONFIDENCE

This chapter takes you through the various emotions that you can run into when giving a presentation. It gives you some key insights and ideas into what causes stage fright and how to channel all that nervous energy into something positive.

You'll learn some very specific techniques that you can apply immediately to reduce stress and present like a pro!

# CHAPTER 2

# YOUR AUDIENCE CRAVES CONFIDENCE

Recognizing that your audience really wants you to be confident is one of life's great revelations and a foundation for your success as a presenter. In this chapter you'll discover the secrets of how to capitalize on this phenomenon and quickly and effortlessly connect with any audience.

# CHAPTER 3

# FAKE IT 'TIL YOU MAKE IT

This chapter takes you through techniques and skills related to mannerisms that you can use right away to project a confident image. A confident image that can be conveyed even if you aren't all that confident!

# CHAPTER 4

# YOUR ROADMAP TO SUCCESS

Chart a course to your own success (every time) by designing a winning presentation using my step-by-step formula.

This chapter shows you how to design and construct your presentation using a proven, foolproof process.

# CHAPTER 5

# VISUALIZE IT!

In this chapter you'll discover the pros and cons of visual aids.

This part of the book takes you into the world of visuals and explains how to use them to keep your audience captivated, and you the presenter, on track.

# CHAPTER 6

# DON'T SWEAT THE DISTRACTING STUFF

Effectively handling stressful situations during your presentation, and keeping your cool, takes real talent.

This chapter gives you invaluable tips on managing the most awkward situations that you're ever likely to face.

# CHAPTER 7

# SELLING YOUR IDEAS

Whether you're selling your ideas to an internal audience, or in a sales situation to a prospect, or to a more general audience, how you do this is crucial to your success. In some ways selling your ideas is just like every other presentation.

In some ways like a few other presentations. In some ways like no other presentation. I'll show you how to sell your ideas, products, or services to have a win win.

# CHAPTER 8

# CROSSING THE VIRTUAL DIVIDE

It's a virtual world. Giving virtual presentations is a fantastic way to share ideas either one-on-one or one-to-many. Your career can be on a trajectory for success when you present with confidence. Zoom/virtual presentations are a wonderful way to exchange ideas, sell your ideas, and sell yourself!

In this Chapter we provide the essential insights into the mission critical things you must put in place in order to succeed.

# CHAPTER 9

# THE CHECKOUT COUNTER

Take away some "ideas at a glance" via these handy, quick-reference checklists. I've boiled down the key ideas in this book into a quick reference guide that you can use as a handy refresher course in advance of all of your future presentations.

# CHAPTER 1

# REPLACING STRESS WITH CONFIDENCE

*"Courage is fear holding on a minute longer".*

- General George S.Patton

# IN THIS CHAPTER...

- Understanding Stage Fright
- Surviving The Experience
- Debunking The Myths Of Body Language
- Developing A Winning Attitude
- Channel Your Nervous Energy For Positive Results

## Monday Morning Blues

It's Monday morning, and you're getting prepared for your presentation. Your script is all set and your presentation materials are ready to go.

Your audience begins to enter the virtual meeting room and you fantasize about how wonderful your presentation will be received. They'll love you. They'll be riveted to your every word. Their sides will split with the jokes you have woven into your presentation. Everything will be perfect. You'll have them eating out of your hand!

All without practicing. All without putting time into crafting the presentation ahead of time or understanding what it takes to put together a truly successful presentation.

Get real! If you believe this, you're in serious need of a reality check! Presenting is an art form. And you, as a presenter are an artist. To be the best that you can be, you have to know your art, the tools of the trade and how to gain the confidence it takes to design, develop and deliver a winning presentation with pizzazz.

Let's take a look at how you can tackle the "art" of presenting and make your vision of being a confident presenter become a reality.

## Sabre Tooth Tigers...And You!

What is stage fright? What is it that makes us blanch and run for cover when we are asked to give a speech? Why don't we relish the prospect of being the center of attention? Hey, when we're out on a Friday night, or sitting around with friends and family at the dining room table or in a pub, we can't wait to get our point across to the group.

So why do we tremble at the thought of doing the same thing in a more formal setting? Well, psychologists have theorized that most of what's happening relates back to suppertime. Suppertime? Yep, suppertime for both saber tooth tigers...and you!

You see, way back when, in prehistoric times, people decided that eating bushes all the time was getting a bit boring. So, people decided that some variety was called for, and they headed off into the deep, dark forest in search of another source of food.

## The Struggle Within

At the same time, sabre tooth tigers were having similar thoughts. They too decided (during a pub night at the local spring) that there might indeed be some tasty morsels out there in the forest that would add variety to their palates. So, they also ventured deep into the dark forest in search of some variety in their diet. And, sooner or later these two seekers of finer fare met...eyeball to eyeball. What happened next impacted the way we think about presentations and speeches forever!

First, they both stopped abruptly and gave each other some rather guarded looks. After looking over each for a nanosecond, each thought the other might make a rather tasty meal. Man, however, became slightly anxious at the sight of this feline monster with overgrown bicuspids. In fact, after further observation, he became downright scared.

However, he resigned himself to the fact that he was going to face this situation head on. He was going to do battle with this beast...he was going to have steak for supper!

Now, what does all this talk about sabre tooth tigers and feline steaks have to do with you as a presenter? Well, guess what, when you're standing in front of an audience, you're mentally preparing yourself for a life or death struggle. You're preparing for the fight of your life. Your audience is, in fact, perceived as the sabre tooth tiger that your ancestors faced. And, in deciding to fight and not flee, you're preparing yourself mentally and physically for the challenge that lies before you.

Mentally, you'll be much more alert. Your senses will be very keen...on guard. As some people observe, you may seen "on edge". You may find yourself talking to yourself just before your presentation. Sizing up your adversary i.e. the audience. How dangerous are they? Why do they look so disinterested? How will they react to you? What if you really screw this up? In your mind, you really are sizing up the enemy. Oh, they may be friendly enough during a normal conversation. But, once they become "the audience", they cease to be the normal people that you had a conversation with just a few moments ago...they become...the potential sabre tooth tiger!

**Physical Changes**

What is happening to you? Well, certain physiological changes take place because of the perceived threat and manifest themselves in different ways because you are indeed unique. The intensity of your emotions will also be quite different than those of your friends or colleagues in a similar situation.

**Different Strokes For Different Folks**

So, changes manifest themselves in different ways for different people. They materialize in varying degrees depending on the audience, your perception of the threat and the situation you find yourself in. For example, a speech given at a wedding is very different from a speech in front of a Board of Directors. However, there are a number of common, physical responses that people experience when they come face-to-face with an audience.

Here are some of the more common ones:

- Weak, wobbly knees–often shaking profusely
- Butterflies in the stomach, or sometimes a very tight knot
- Hot, flushed feeling in your cheeks
- Visibly trembling hands
- Sweaty palms
- Palpitating heart–you can feel and see it pounding
- Dry throat. BTW. That's why experienced speakers have a glass of water handy
- Quivering voice – yes, a very noticeable tremor in your voice

Sweat! Sweat! Sweat!

All in all, you can become a physical wreck when confronted with a public speaking situation. In fact, sometimes people start to feel and exhibit these emotions just thinking about giving a speech.

Why is this happening to you? It's happening because you're normal! When facing an audience, you are no longer a part of a group that offers security. When you face your audience, you usually face them alone. As such, you feel alone and very, very, vulnerable.

This is, in fact, one of the keys to understanding the fears most associated with public speaking.

Let's examine it further.

Imagine you're sitting at a table having an "adult beverage" with six or seven of your colleagues or friends. The discussion is flowing smoothly and everyone is conversing quite naturally. You feel absolutely no tension or anxiety when you speak. In fact, during the conversation, you sometimes have trouble holding back from "cutting off" the other person before they have finished expressing themselves.

However, imagine that you are now asked to stand up and make a brief presentation to the very same people that a moment before you were sipping a cool one with. Yes, the very same people with whom you have just engaged in a lively discussion. Are you beginning to feel nervous? Are you getting anxious? You rise to speak and push your chair away. You feel like crawling under the table. You get a sinking feeling in the pit of your stomach. You might even feel nauseated.

What on earth is going on? What's changed? What's happened to cause all of this anxiety? Why would you suddenly experience stage fright in front of your friends or colleagues?

**You Are No Longer Part Of The Group!**

Simply put, you are no longer part of the group and the security it provides. You have separated yourself physically and mentally, and they also have from you. You have a new role to play, you're more vulnerable, and you have to "go it alone".

There is also another dimension to this situation. From a presentation perspective, you have switched from a "conversational mode" to a "presentation mode". When you were having a drink with your colleagues, the onus wasn't on you (or any other individual) to carry the conversation. As a matter of fact, you didn't have any responsibility to the group to contribute to any part of the conversation.

When you rise to give a presentation, everything changes. Let's drill down.

## The Sound Of Silence

When you're giving a presentation the onus is entirely on you to "discuss" something. If you don't say anything, there will be nothing but the sound of silence in the room. This is very uncomfortable for your audience and you. You know intuitively that you have a responsibility to the group. In fact, in the role of being presenter, you have the responsibility to carry on a one-way conversation. Your audience is looking to you and only to you.

For most people this creates a strong sense of discomfort, in fact it can make you feel downright nervous.

## Scared Stiff!

Your nervousness is usually associated with a number of fear factors that can creep into your mind when you are asked to give a speech. These fears are often based upon events of the past or can be the result of perceived threats posed by your audience. Here are two of the major fears associated with speaking in front of an audience:

- You're the focus of attention and it's nerve wracking!

This is a basic fear for most people when they're the focus of attention. What if something goes terribly wrong? What if the computer fails? What if you can't remember what you're supposed to say? Just how will you react to these challenges in front of your audience?

- There is also the fear of outright rejection!

In essence, you really want to be accepted by your audience. Therefore, one of the things that you fear the most is, in fact, rejection from the group. All of this is compounding the perceived risks when you're in front of any audience.

## And There's More!

There is one additional fear or risk you may experience if you find yourself speaking in front of some of your colleagues from work. The way you "handle yourself" in front of your co-workers may, you feel, have a fundamental effect on the future of your job and career. If you're timid and nervous, it could have a negative impact on the manner in which you are perceived by your boss, your subordinates and your peers. And this perception could have an impact on their view of your ability to handle and manage other aspects of your job and career.

However, if your presentation is a success, it can work wonders to improve your image in the eyes of your boss! Your self-esteem will get a boost. And your presentation might have a fantastic, positive impact on your chances for promotion and even fast track you to a new phase in your career!

So far, we've explored a number of reasons why people are nervous in front of an audience. Now, it's time to take a brief look at some common results of this nervousness, and some concrete things that you can do to help yourself.

When looking at physiological changes that happen to people who make presentations it is extremely important to remember that this is something that happens to most speakers from time to time. So, let's cut to the chase.

**The Infamous Butterflies In Your Stomach!**

Your gut can be turned upside down because of a pending presentation. When we talk about "the butterflies" it means that your super-sensitive digestive system is being thrown into a topsy-turvy imbalance because of your nervousness.

What can you do to counter this? Well, you have a number of options. Some people find that it's best not to eat anything prior to their presentation. Others find it best to eat so that they "have something in their stomach." Whichever remedy is right for you, it's probably best not to overeat when you feel in a panic over your presentation. This is just asking for trouble! So, accept the butterflies, they will go away.

**I Think I'm Blushing!**

Another phenomenon that can afflict you is the sensation of blushing. This, for many people, is an automatic reaction to what is perceived as a potentially embarrassing situation. Oh, sure enough, you have yet to actually be embarrassed, but the sheer thought of it can lead you to blush. The key to coping with this is to "get over it!" If you are blushing, so what? You are aware of this, but not necessarily your audience. In fact, when conducting workshops on presentation techniques, I've often played back video recordings of people who had presented and thought they were blushing. More often than not this was something that wasn't noticeable to their audience.

So, if you think you are blushing, chances are that it isn't visible. You may feel a warm or hot sensation in your face. This does not mean, however, that it will manifest itself into a full blown "blush".

Also, a reddening of the neck may be something that will happen to you from time to time, and that's AOK. You can easily overcome this by simply wearing a high fitting shirt collar or wearing a high-collared sweater or turtleneck undershirt if appropriate. It's that simple!

**The Shaky Hands**

You may find that your hands also take on a mind of their own and decide to have a free-for-all in the form a "trembling fit" in front of your audience. If so, here are a few things that you can keep in mind to tackle this situation:

- It's usually temporary. It will probably stop after a few minutes, so wait it out.
- Gesture naturally, and get your hands moving to wear off the shakes (some people call this gesticulating).
- Don't do things that will draw attention to your shaky hands such as holding a glass of water or pointing to a visual aid with your shaky finger.

**Heart Throb**

Yes, suddenly you realize that you really do have a heart. In fact, you're very aware of your heart for maybe the very first time in your life. Your heart, that wonderful pump that just keeps on ticking, has developed a beat that puts rap music to shame. In fact, your ticker may feel like it is about to jump out of your chest! The bottom-line is that your heart is palpitating.

Take 5 deep breaths, it really will help you to cope with this situation. Plus, try to condition yourself mentally by telling yourself to relax. Think calm, think yoga. Tell yourself to slow everything down to clear your mind. The stress is real, but you can do something "real" about it.

**Your Throat Feels Like The Sands Of The Sahara**

Okay, you are about to begin to speak, and you suddenly realize that your throat is parched. You try to swallow, but you have nothing to swallow. You couldn't spit if your life depended on it.

Try to do what the "pros'" do and have a glass of water handy. Pause to take a drink whenever you feel the urge. In fact, pause to take a drink even if you don't have the urge! A drink of water will not only cure your parched throat instantly it will also demonstrate poise and composure to your audience.

Take a look at the talk shows on TV. All of them, yes, all of them have a glass of water or a cup of coffee for the host and guest to drink from. Why? Because it can let the speaker cure the parched throat, gather their thoughts while doing this, and look cool and relaxed when they do it. Additionally, if you don't have water handy, try to simply force a swallow. It won't happen that often that it looks painfully evident to your audience, but it will get some lubricant into your vocal cords.

Quite often you'll find that a dry throat is in fact a temporary problem and will often disappear in a few minutes.

**A Voice In The Wilderness**

Picture this. You're all alone and in the spotlight on a ZOOM call. You open your mouth to begin your presentation. And, what comes out is terrifying! You have a quivering, shaking, trembling voice that projects the image of someone who is absolutely terrified at being in this situation.

This affliction hits most of us at some point in our speech making endeavors. Usually it strikes us right at the very beginning of a speech. Sometimes, however, it plagues us throughout our entire presentation. What can you do?

Here are some key pointers that should help you cope with, or overcome, this extremely nerve-racking phenomenon:

- Increase the volume of your voice. Confident presenters speak with authority. An audience usually interprets a person who has a louder than normal voice as someone who projects confidence. Try this and you will also feel more confident and override the quiver in your voice.
- Accept it as part of the beginning of a presentation and work your way through it. Quite often it will dissipate as you get into your presentation.
- Take a drink of water and lubricate your vocal cords. As

mentioned before, having a drink of water gives you a chance to gain your composure, and your trembling voice will also often disappear.

- Engage in "small talk" with people in your audience before you start your presentation. This will a) warm up your vocal cords b) give you a chance to break the ice with people in the audience and c) get you in the right frame of mind to simply engage in a natural form of conversation when you begin speaking to the entire audience.

**Don't Sweat The Small Stuff...Like Your Sweaty Palms**

Ninety-five percent of people who give speeches have sweaty palms before they start. The other five percent get cold hands. So live with it, either way you're normal.

Yes, sweating before and during a presentation is very normal. It is sometimes more pronounced in some people than others. What to do?

Try a couple of these ideas to mitigate this common problem:

- Use an industrial strength deodorant! Don't overlook this. Even if you're alone will boost your confidence. Also, you'll smell wonderful!
- Wear a jacket or sweater to hide perspiration on your shirt or blouse. There's nothing worse or more distracting than a presenter who has underarm perspiration marks. You just plain don't need the additional worry.

Have some Kleenex handy if you normally perspire a lot. You can always wipe your brow and relieve the pressure this way.

Bottom line? Prepare ahead of time, and don't sweat it!

When you're giving a presentation, you'll often find that your body is having some weird and unnatural reactions similar to one (or all!) of the points we've just covered.

Our difficulty often lies not in having these things physical things actually happen to us, but in our reaction to what is happening to us. We often overestimate the reaction we think the audience is having to us. We tend to be oversensitive to what's happening to us and believe that the audience is also extremely sensitive and distracted by this.

However, it's usually only you, the presenter, who will notice to any large degree these physical changes. Why? You're so attuned to your body that you're extremely sensitive to any changes that are manifested. Unfortunately, we often let this play on our emotions, and this really can exacerbate the situation to the detriment of our presentations. Remember, the audience is not as sensitized to how you normally sound or act, and these changes are usually barely perceptible to your audience, if at all.

The crucial point to keep in mind is that you are probably the only person in the room who will notice some of these physical reactions. Don't fall into the trap of allowing yourself to be oversensitive.

**Fast Talk**

If you're feeling anxious about your presentation there's often a natural tendency to speak at a rate that's really faster than normal. I'm not sure if it's because presenters want to just plain get the hell out of there or not, but it is quite common!

You may experience, therefore, a dramatic increase in the speed at which you're speaking. You have suddenly become a motor mouth! You sound like a runaway train. Your audience (hanging on for dear life) is trying not to let go of what you are saying as you careen through the various twists and turns of your presentation.

And you, determined to get through this, take them all on a twisting, turning, pedal-to-the-metal car ride that they'll never forget. Needless to say, the effectiveness of this type of presentation style leaves a lot to be desired.

The solution? Tell yourself to slow down!! Write down somewhere in your notes or cue cards (or anywhere handy if you're not using notes) the words "SLOW DOWN". You have to be strict with yourself so you won't speak too quickly. You'll often be so wrapped up in your presentation that you just keep going at warp speed. You need to put speed bumps at some strategic points in your presentation that will remind you to slow your pace down to a reasonable level. Write down these words in key places so that you have a constant reminder not to rush the pace. Relax, and let your passengers enjoy the ride with you.

A word of caution. Ensure that you have enough time to get your message and points across in the time that's been allotted. Otherwise, you may find yourself naturally rushing to make sure that you "get through" all your presentation material. How will you know how long it will take? Simple. Practice with a watch in front of you. It's absolutely the best way to get a fairly accurate idea of just how long your presentation will take.

Another example of a way to judge the time required to do the presentation is to count the number of key points in your presentation and make a rough guess at how long it will take to deliver each point. If you have fifty points written down and your guess is about one minute per point, you'll need approximately 50 minutes to deliver your ideas. Please note: this doesn't include any questions from your audience.

**Do You Have Distracting Behaviors?**

Many of us develop some extremely unnatural, distracting

behaviors when we're facing an audience in a virtual presentation. Here's just a sampling of some that you may have seen, or exhibited, from time to time:

- Fumbling or playing with
- Paper clips
- Notes
- Pen tops
- Rings on fingers
- Nervous wringing of your hands
- Rubbing your hands on your nose/face

Often, you'll be unaware that you're engaged in these types of behaviors. However, once you are aware of the potential problems associated with these nervous habits, there are a few simple, yet effective, techniques that you can use to address them. Here are some ideas to keep in mind.

Have you developed any of these distracting habits? One way to find out is to ask someone to watch you during a practice session, or during an actual presentation, and ask them to specifically look for these traits. When they give you feedback, be sure to accept it graciously, i.e., don't get defensive.

Another valuable thing that you can do is to videotape yourself during a practice or live presentation and then critique it after the fact. You may be surprised at what you discover!

Get rid of distracting habits and adopt positive ones. Your confidence will grow.

**Fillers**

When you're nervous you may also develop the annoying yet

common habit of inserting words or phrases that are used as "fillers" between your thoughts. Just a few common examples are the ubiquitous "ok", "ya know", "like", or just plain "ah" or "um".

A few of these sprinkled in a speech are considered natural. However, they can become extremely irritating and annoying if you use them to excess.

Here's what to do:

- If you are giving an in-person presentation ask a friend in the audience to give you a secret signal every time you use one of these fillers (understanding that they may not be a friend for long after they've signaled you 100 times!)
- Review a video of your presentation and count the number of times that you use the word "Ok" or any other word you tend to over use.
- Say the filler inaudibly during your presentation so that only you can hear it. I used to do this, and it really satisfied my psychological need to add the filler word until I no longer needed it.
- Say the filler mentally to yourself. Only you will know that you used one. Once again, this satisfies a psychological need to say it.
- Be a strict taskmaster with yourself. When you want to use a filler word, just say no!
- Write a note in your presentation notes, and simply say "No Ok"! You may need this kind of reminder as you get caught up in the heat of your presentation.

Realize that a brief pause between sentences or thoughts is in fact very professional. It gives your audience time to digest what you've said and prepares them for your next idea. Watch some of the "pros" do this to great effect.

## Body Language: What Is It Your Audience Is Telling You?

I've read numerous books over the years that have focused on understanding and interpreting the non-verbal messages sent to us via body language. Pundits try to propagate the myth that they understand what a person is thinking by simply observing how they hold their hands. I am not a believer.

In truth, there are occasions when you can tell what a person is thinking. For example, if they clench their fist and then punch you in the nose, chances are that their body language is telling you that they don't like you very much. IMHO everything else short of that is mere speculation!

What is body language? It's the non-verbal behavior that we can observe in another person, behavior that might provide insights into the feelings or attitudes a person is experiencing at a given moment in time. And, if you're checking out the audience for clues as to how you're doing, you may find it very disconcerting indeed.

For example, you might observe a person tapping or drumming their fingers on a table. This non-verbal behavior could indicate that the person is somewhat frustrated or impatient. They want you to "get on with it"! He or she wouldn't have to say anything to reflect their frustration because their fingers are sending you this message quite clearly. Or are they?

Does this kind of behavior (drumming one's fingers on a table) always reflect frustration or impatience? Is it always an indication of what the person is feeling at that moment about your presentation? Of course not. It could be their way of mulling over or thinking about what you are saying. Or, they could be thinking about something totally different at that time and not even listening to you (perish the thought)!

All too often when we're making a speech we are super sensitive to the non-verbal behavior of certain members of the audience. We're often too quick to jump to the wrong conclusions about the body language messages that are being transmitted and far too quick to interpret these messages in a negative way.

### How You Can be Misled by Body Language

Let me share with you just one example of how I was totally misled by the body language of an individual in my audience. I was giving a presentation to about forty people in a business setting. The presentation centered on the introduction of an exciting new idea that would make this particular company a leader in its field. However, one member of the audience was obviously not convinced of the merits of the idea.

How did I know? Well, it wasn't that he said anything negative throughout the presentation. But I knew! You see, I could tell his attitude by his body language. Here's what I observed about him during my one-hour presentation.

- He was slumped in his chair
- He had his arms folded across his chest at all times
- He was extremely inattentive, i.e., he looked around the room, or stared at the table in front of him
- He wore a constant frown on his face
- He never smiled or joined in the laughter of others when something spontaneously funny happened

My interpretation of his body language? He obviously couldn't wait for the presentation to finish so that he could get out of there as quickly as possible. And, in fact, when the presentation was finished he bolted out of the room.

Was I unsettled, bothered, and a little ticked by this? You bet.

I was sure, by his actions, that he hated me at first sight and thought the entire presentation was a waste of his time and was extremely bored.

After focusing in on his negative behavior for over an hour, these were the only logical conclusions that I could come to.

Was I right? No. I was about as wrong as I could be. How do I know? Well, here's the rest of the story.

I was hurt and angry, okay, as mentioned...actually ticked off! And, as I was gathering up my notes and other presentation materials for the flight home I was really "stewing" over this person's attitude.

Everyone in the audience had left. Suddenly, the door at the back of the meeting room swung open. There he was! He strutted boldly to the front of the room, stopped and extended his hand. We shook hands. Then he said very calmly, "Thanks. That's the best damned presentation we've had here in ten years." Then he smiled, turned around and left the room.

My jaw hit the ground! I couldn't believe my eyes or ears. How could this be? How could I have been this wrong? How could he have been sitting there, looking so surly, yet thinking such positive thoughts?

Fortunately, this event took place early in my career and taught me a very valuable lesson that I'll never forget, i.e., don't be too sensitive to the behavior or reactions that you observe in certain members of the audience. When you are giving a presentation and observe a seemingly negative reaction, stay calm, cool and collected. Keep on smiling. Some people in your audience may be sending you a message that you're apt to misinterpret.

And, these days, more often than not you will see on video calls people looking at a device or around at other information on there screen. Just ignore this and keep going. It's hard to do but realize it is often just there habit of multi-tasking.

This doesn't mean that we shouldn't be aware and sensitive to the responses in some members of the audience. Sometimes, we can use these behaviors to correctly interpret people's feelings. However, ensure that you don't become pre-occupied or oversensitive to body language. You may be wrong!

**Does Being Nervous Make You More Nervous...Let's Be Realistic**

My hands start to sweat about fifteen minutes before I give a presentation. My hands have always started to sweat fifteen minutes before a presentation, they probably always will.

How do I cope with this reaction? It's simply my attitude towards my hands sweating that helps me to cope.
Many years ago, I would get terribly upset with myself when I started to react nervously with sweaty hands and the occasional knot in my stomach, before giving a presentation.

Not any more. Now, I'm able to put this nervousness into perspective. In fact, I expect to have sweaty palms. And, because I expect it, I don't get upset over it when it happens. I'm able to look at what's physically happening to me and say, "Hey, that's OK, it's just me and it's normal."

**Stomach Gets Knots**

At one point in time I had to give a speech at City Hall. About a hundred neighbors were gathered to support a motion to purchase some land for a neighborhood park. I was asked to be their spokesperson... lucky me. I had been conducting seminars on presentation skills for some time, and so was well prepared for the speech to the city councilors. I was psyched up for the event, had a terrific support group behind me, and was all set to go.

However, I was in for quite a surprise. I suddenly got a very painful knot in my stomach. It got tighter and tighter, and bigger and bigger. Indeed, it was actually physically quite painful.

I hadn't experienced a knot in my stomach like this for many years. And it caught me completely by surprise. For a second or two I started to wonder just how nervous I really was! However, I stopped this negative way of thinking very quickly and said to myself, "How about that. A knot in my stomach. I didn't expect it but it is there. So what! I'm all set to go, get on with it, and do the best you can."

The lesson? Although I didn't expect to have this kind of nervous reaction, when it did happen, I was able to put it into perspective and not let it upset me. You too can learn to put this kind of physiological reaction into perspective. If your hands are sweaty, your stomach is in a knot, your knees are a little wobbly, you too can deal with it and get over it! Learn to look at these reactions in a very objective and emotionless way. You'll be surprised at just how much easier it becomes when you can learn to do this and accept these physical manifestations of nervousness.

P.S. We got a beautiful park in our neighborhood.

**Stage Fright is Normal and Yes You Can Get Over It!**

Stage fright is normal. It's something that you and every other presenter on planet earth experiences and learns to live with. Your nervousness may manifest itself in various ways (and degrees) depending on the audience or circumstances. You can, however, learn to minimize its impact and cope with its effects.

We've already looked at many ways of tackling the problem of nervousness. During the remainder of this book you'll discover other exciting ways of overcoming stage fright. And, you'll learn how to create a truly enjoyable and worthwhile speech or presentation for both you and your audience.

However, please don't ever expect to be as comfortable giving a speech as you are when you're say watching TV or in a pub. You should always feel that twinge of nervousness, that rush of adrenaline, that air of excitement. It's a good thing(:

I remember in the past, when I was extremely nervous, I used to admire some of the great actors and actresses who handled television interviews so impressively. I was amazed when many of them expressed how nervous they were when accepting an Academy Award. In fact, I was not only amazed, I thought they were lying to us for effect and being just plain phony. How could these superstars of the big screen, so skilled at acting and performing, feel nervous about giving a two-minute acceptance speech? Did these superstars really expect me to believe that they were nervous?

Yes. You see, they really were nervous. And, that's to their credit. Why? Because it shows that they really do care about the people in their audience and how they come across as presenters. They, like you and I, care about doing a good job.

If they ever lose sight of their all-important audience, then that's when they'll no longer be nervous. And, that's when they'll start to lose perspective of what success is all about. It's all about the audience, not them. Always.

Remember, being nervous is normal and something that happens naturally to all of us. So, if you're nervous, it's AOK. Be assured, however, that you can learn how to reduce the effects of nervousness using some of the ideas we've explored so that you'll actually enjoy making a speech. You'll be able to relax and speak with confidence.

In the next chapter we'll look at how your audience can impact your presentation's success. And show you how to feel good about being in front of any audience so that you can become a truly confident presenter.

# CHAPTER 2

# YOUR AUDIENCE CRAVES CONFIDENCE!

"Whatever course you decide upon, there is always someone to tell you that you are wrong. There are always difficulties arising, which tempt you to believe that your critics are right. To map out a course of action and follow it to an end requires courage. "

**-Ralph Waldo Emerson**

# IN THIS CHAPTER...

- Exploring Your Audience's Needs
- Profiling Your Audience
- Making the Connection
- Getting them Engaged

## They Love Me... They Love Me Not

Some years ago, when I was petrified at the very thought of giving presentations, I worried a lot about the audience I was about to face. Even if I knew them well. Even if I didn't.

Here's what would typically take place. The people would casually enter the meeting room, strolling and chatting amongst themselves. I would immediately (and quite naturally), start to make judgments as to their character and personality. There, sitting in a refined posture, would be a sophisticated gentleman in his late forties with a blue pin striped suit, graying around the temples, confident and charismatic. I would think to myself. "Wow! This guy has been around. I'm way out of his league! What the hell is he doing here listening to me?"

In another part of the room, there would be a group of young rebels, who were aggressive, talkative and full of their own self-importance. Not much younger than I was, but obviously waiting in the bushes to leap for my jugular if I gave even the slightest hint of falling short of their unrealistic expectations.

Then, there were the women in the audience. How would they react to me? What if I screwed up and said something that sounded really chauvinistic even though I am not?

Can you relate to these thoughts of self-doubt? Do you size up the audience to your disadvantage? Will you mess up your presentation because you've messed up in your head? How can one presenter handle and cope with all these different personalities, genders and age levels?

Well, you really can cope with all these different variables. Not only can you cope, you can learn to look at an audience in a way that you've never quite looked at one before. You see, you need to understand that the entire audience is made up of people who are very similar to you. People who have the same kinds of feelings and emotions as you have. People who put their shoes on one foot at a time. They're just ordinary people. And, because of that, there's one thing that you can always rely on that should boost your confidence. They're usually on your side!

That's right. Please go back and read the last statement five times. Etch it in your memory forever.

**The Audience Wants You To Be A Winner!**

It took me ages to accept the simple truth that the audience wasn't against me. In fact, not only were they not against me, they really wanted me to do an outstanding job of being a presenter! And that's the difference between the old me as a presenter, and the new me. The old me thought that the audience was comprised of people who wanted me to fail, wanted me to end up with the proverbial egg all over my face.

But, after a while, I turned all of this around and realized that the extreme opposite was true. What they really wanted was for me to succeed. They wanted to have a winner in front of them.

How can you be certain that this is true for you also? You'll know that it will hold true for you if you can just reflect on your responses as a member of an audience. For me, I began by getting in touch with my feelings i.e., the feelings I had when I was watching someone else give a speech.

What did I discover? Interestingly enough I found that I really was pulling for the presenter. I really did want him or her to do well. If the presenter was obviously "terrified", I found myself really and truly hoping that person would make it through this obviously trying ordeal. Hoping beyond hope that there would be no stalling or stumbling. Secretly wanting to encourage the presenter to "hang in there". I did not want that person to fail.

**It's The Same All Over**

I started to discuss openly my responses and feelings about this with some of my colleagues who had been in the audience with me when someone was obviously nervous. I discovered that they too felt empathy and support for the nervous presenter. They too, very much, wanted the presenter to be more confident and relaxed.

Slowly at first, then like a lightning bolt, I realized it's human nature for people in our audiences to want us to succeed. They want us to look and act confident. They want us to feel very comfortable in front of them.

Why? I'm not completely sure about all the Freudian reasons behind all of this, but I do have a couple of theories. First, I believe many people have been through the very same emotional experiences themselves. They've felt the stress and anxiety associated with giving a presentation. They want to reach out to the presenter and say, "It's okay. I understand. I've been in your shoes. You have nothing to fear." And, because they can relate to the experience and associated feelings, they feel an emotional bond between themselves and the presenter.

I also believe that, deep down, some members of the audience may actually feel an overwhelming feeling of guilt when a speaker is nervous. You see, they feel that they are the ones responsible for making the presenter so anxious. They are culpable. So, in order to rid themselves of this guilt, they want the presenter to be more confident. They start saying things to themselves such as, "I don't know why he's so nervous, after all, it's only us."

## Lighten Up!

We could spend a lot of wasted time and effort psychoanalyzing this whole fear of presenting phenomena. However, I don't believe that it would help. No matter what psychological reasons are at the root cause for these feelings, the one fact remains that your audience is on your side. They want you to act and feel comfortable in front of them so that they can also relax.

You can cause them a lot of stress if you're looking at them as if they're some kind of lynch mob. It's akin to watching a comedian. We really do want them to be funny. We really want him or her to succeed and make us laugh. The same holds true for an audience when you're presenting. They want you to do well.

So, put it all into perspective. People feel comfortable around confident people. Give them what they really and truly want. Show them that you are confident. Give them the impression that you're confident and they'll relax and love you for it. Lighten up!

## The Exception Makes The Rule

Ok, I know what you're thinking. You're saying to yourself, "Oh sure, how naive can you get?" Not everybody I know wants me to succeed. Not everyone is really hoping that I do well. In fact I know some people who probably can't stand me and want to see me fail".

You're absolutely right. There will be the odd exception. Those one or two people in the audience, who, for whatever warped reasons, may nurture a negative thought or two. Maybe they're jealous of someone who looks so confident. Maybe they've been told by their boss to attend your presentation against their wishes. Maybe you have a personality conflict with them. Maybe, maybe, maybe. But, by-and-large, ninety nine percent of the people you present to really and truly hope that you succeed. They honestly want you to do well. So, concentrate on the positive people in your audience. They'll be glad you did.

And, of course, if you are presenting to a hostile audience because of the stand you and your colleagues may be taking it will be more challenging. Examples abound at City Hall meetings where people are at odds with each other on a certain issue. In cases like this, it is crucial that you set your expectations appropriately and realize that it is the message and not the messenger that they are opposing. Let's explore that further next.

**Show Some Class!**

I know, I know, it's hard when someone is looking at us with a scowl on his or her face. However, my friend, don't you dare give up on these types so quickly. You have a unique opportunity to show yourself in a different light to them. An opportunity to show some class.

Here's an example that may help to illustrate my point. How would you handle an audience that you know will be really ticked off with what you're telling them? People who are going to be affected in some detrimental way by your message? For example, "You'll have to work harder with less pay". Yikes! One can hardly expect these folks to be on your side.

Or, can you? Try to remember, that although from time to time you may have to tell people some unpleasant or controversial news, it's the "message" that they are attacking and reacting to, not you. As long as you can keep this in mind, you will be able to face a relatively antagonistic crowd in a more understanding, objective and confident manner. Try to understand their feelings and appreciate their reasons for expressing their anger or disappointment.

**You Want Us To Do What?!**

Another example that causes presenters to be very concerned about an audience is when the presenter asks for a commitment from them. Imagine you are a manager, and you're requesting approval from an Executive Committee to add three additional people to complete an on-going business project that is running behind schedule. Chances are you're going to meet a lot of challenges and questions related to this request. Challenges that you may misinterpret as aggression on the part of certain audience members, members who are being asked to weigh the merits of your request and make a decision.

If you pause for a minute and think about the situation the audience is in, you'll soon realize that the audience is simply doing their job. A job that requires them to challenge you and probe many aspects of your presentation in order to assure themselves that the decision they make is a sound and justifiable one.

In essence, it is the audience's role to discover the value of granting your request. It's your role to conduct the presentation and convey the information in a professional manner that will enable them to make a knowledge-based decision. This will, quite naturally, involve some intense questioning on the part of these "decision makers".

It's crucial when you face such an audience to ensure that you don't misinterpret their questions and seemingly antagonistic behavior as aggression. Don't allow yourself to fall into the trap of letting your emotions get in the way of clearly presenting the facts. Remember, although the audience in a situation like this may seem to be totally against you, they're not. They are fulfilling their role by challenging your ideas, and that's okay.

In conclusion, whenever you're concerned about addressing an audience, remember to put the whole situation into perspective. Look to your own expectations of the audience and what their reaction will likely be to your presentation. Is it an upbeat, informative topic where many folks may benefit from the information? Or, conversely, is the topic such that you can expect some controversy and challenges?

Either way, think about your audience ahead of time. Prepare yourself for this mentally. And remember, most of the time they really are on your side.

**There's Some Strangers In The Crowd! Does It Matter?**

At one point in my life I was very comfortable with audiences where I knew each of the audience members. They were often people I worked with every day. But, if I had to face a room full of strangers, I panicked! Is that what you're like? Or, are you like some people I've met in my presentation skills seminars who are just the opposite? They're comfortable with a room full of strangers, but dread facing people who they know or work with.

Another problem that plagued me early in my career was the size of the audience. I'd feel very comfortable with an audience of ten people or less. However, if the size got up into the high teens or more, I'd want to run and hide.

How do I feel now? I relish a crowd of a hundred or more! Now, I don't care if they are friends, colleagues or strangers.

How did I overcome these common fears? What can you do to feel more comfortable in front of any size audience? How can you relax in front of friends or strangers? Let's take a closer look.

## What's Your Audience's Credit Rating?

What is the secret sauce? Give your audience credit. That's right, credit. Credit that they will like you right away. Credit that they will be on your side. Credit that they are basically ordinary people who will be courteous, interested and even enjoy your presentation. Give them this credit before you start your presentation, before you even open your mouth!

When did I start to get all of these positive feelings about an audience? Come along with me and take a journey back in time, to a time when I first started to conduct presentations.

My first presentations were to small groups of approximately five people. These people were usually at a middle management level, and the presentations were conducted in fairly informal business settings. At first I was extremely "stressed out". Stressed at the very thought of conducting these presentations. I'd lay awake the night before a presentation, wondering if I would remember everything that I wanted to tell the audience members. I was overly concerned about the way I'd be accepted by these people who were much more experienced and older than I was. Maybe you can relate to staying awake half the night with similar fears!

During my first few fledgling presentations I was so nervous that I just wanted to get through them and get the hell out of there. After a while, however, I found myself being extremely nervous at the beginning of a presentation but at the end I felt "pretty good". I won't go so far as to say I enjoyed them, but at the end I did feel a real sense of reward and accomplishment.

This pattern (nervous at the start, feeling good at the conclusion of a presentation) continued for many years. Along the way, I had the good fortune to present to a variety of audiences. Some, small groups of between five and ten people, and some many times that size. Sometimes I would know everybody in the audience, sometimes a few people, and sometimes not a single person.

I did notice, however, that no matter what the audience's mix or size, the feelings I had were consistent. I'd go into the presentation with lots of self-doubt and anxiety. My exit feelings were totally opposite. I would be buoyed up by the experience and have a high regard for the people in the audience.

After a while, I began to take a closer, more objective look at the pattern that had evolved. I was getting extremely frustrated at being nervous before conducting my presentations. I'd become a fairly experienced and seasoned presenter and actually looked forward to presenting.

Except? Except for the initial five minutes or so when my guts were churning and my voice was quivering to the point of embarrassment. I had to find a way out of this "mess". Something had to be done.

## If You Think You Can't ...You're Right.

What did I do to get off of this on-going roller coaster? I started to think that I could get off of it if I could just find the "silver bullet". And, the silver bullet was sitting right in front of me in my ammo box. You see, after really thinking about this pattern for a long time, I came to the realization that I wasn't allowing myself the confidence to recognize that all audiences were really on my side from the very start of my presentation.

After this realization, I kept testing my theory, looking for signs of acceptance. As I received more and more of these indicators of acceptance during the course of my presentations, my confidence began to skyrocket. At a certain point, during the early stages of giving a presentation, I had enough signs of acceptance that I began to relax, began to accept the fact that the audience accepted me.

This was a new attitude that was to change my feelings about all audiences for the rest of my life.

## Take The Weight Off Your Shoulders... Right From The Start

I decided, in one bold move, not to wait for signs of acceptance before I allowed myself to feel comfortable in front of an audience. I gave myself permission to act and feel as comfortable as I did during the latter part of my previous presentations. This took a tremendous amount of stress off me.

This new attitude has enabled me to approach a multitude of presentation situations with the utmost confidence. Confidence based on experience after experience that indicated to me that all audiences were basically the same. People want us to be relaxed. Not relaxed halfway through a presentation, not relaxed at the end of a presentation, but confident and relaxed from the "get go".

If you can also start to think about it in this way you can truly begin to enjoy and relish the experience of giving any and all presentations, on any topic, anywhere and to any audience.

Does this mean that you'll still experience some anxiety about conducting presentations? Sure you will. However, it's the same anxiety that's felt by all athletes before "the big game" or race. It will manifest itself because you (like these athletes) want to do your "personal best" every time you're out in front of an audience. This is, in fact, a very positive attitude and attribute. Look forward to the challenge!

Give yourself permission to look and feel confident from the moment you utter your opening remarks. Give your audience the credit to accept you as a presenter. They really do want you to succeed. They want you to feel comfortable so that they can feel comfortable. How do I know? Because your audiences are the same as my audiences, comprised of ordinary people like you and me.

## Who's Who In The Zoo?

Try to get acquainted with your audience before you formally face them in order to develop a profile of them. Why is this important to your success? Well, your confidence will automatically increase if you can start to form a visual image of the audience in your mind's eye. You'll be well prepared to meet them and address their needs and expectations. Use the following guidelines:

### How Large An Audience Can You Expect?

Find out how many people will be in your audience. This will help you to visualize the audience before you face them and at the same time help you to relax and increase your confidence.

### Who Will Be In Your Audience?

This information will provide you with invaluable insights that will be extremely useful when you're developing the content of your presentation. You want to ensure that your presentation material targets your audience's unique needs as a group.

### What Roles Do They Have?

Having this information will allow you to inject some thoughts or ideas that will allow you to "connect" directly with them as individuals. I can't stress enough how important this is as it relates to your confidence and success of your presentation!!

## Group Think ... A Deeper Dive

What does your audience have in common as a group? Try to determine what the key link is amongst the members of your audience? Is it a community service group made up of volunteers? Is it a particular department within an organization? Is it a special interest group with a common purpose?

Whatever the link is, try to identify it and work references to it into your presentation. Build a link into the introductory portion of your presentation to ensure that each person realizes that they will be able to identify with the content. In essence, seek out and find the common bond that brings your audience together.

For example, a touring concert singer in your hometown might say. "Hey, (fill in your hometown name), it's great to be here tonight!" The performer wants to express his or her appreciation to you, the audience, for coming out to hear the concert and wants to convey the message that you're special.

Usually, the audience goes wild at the mere mention of their city! These entertainers know the value and power of connecting with their audience with something they ALL have in common. Right from the outset.

Here are a few examples that further illustrate this point:

- If it's a service group, you might reference some of the many community projects that the club members have successfully completed that they are particularly proud of.
- A particular department within a larger organization will, no doubt, have a mission or goal you can reference.
- Special interest groups (e.g. conservationists) may have a cause or special project that they can identify with.

If you inject into your presentation some references to these common, relatable links, you'll convey to your audience that you identify with them. You recognize the bond that brings them together, and you want to be part of that special relationship that they have in common.

This is how you can start to establish that all-important, yet so elusive, rapport with any audience.

Here's a handy **Top Ten Checklist** of questions you can use to help you to identify with your audience and focus on their needs:

1. Does the audience already know something about the subject matter you're presenting?

2. Why should they be interested in your topic?

3. Does each individual in the audience know as much about the topic as the person sitting next to them?

4. What event in the recent past can they all relate to?

5. Is there any terminology or acronyms you're planning on using that they may not understand and should be explained?

6. Will they be able to understand how the information you're discussing will impact them and in what way?

7. Can you expect any objections? What will they likely be? Be prepared with a rebuttal.

8. Are there any "taboo" subjects? (I ALWAYS ask this one. I have too may scars from when I forgot to ask!)

9. Are there any reporting relationships or is there anyone "special" in the audience?

10. What are the "hot" issues for this group?

You can ask these questions of the presentation organizer to try to find out as much as you can about your audience and what will RESONATE with them. Then, build into your content some ideas that will enable you to meet your audience's expectations.

If you do this, your confidence, and their appreciation of you as a presenter, can only go one way, straight up! Your audience's expectations of your presentation is crucial in the win-win scenario. Let's take a closer look.

**What Counts? Your Audience's Expectations!**

What are their expectations? Find out what your audience wants to "get" out of your presentation. Should it be humorous, serious, entertaining or educational? Or, all of the above?

Make sure you know what the audience members are being told ahead of time about your presentation. This is also crucial to your success/confidence formula. You want to ensure that you'll meet their expectations.

This last point, related to meeting expectations, deserves some very special attention. For example, you may be invited as a guest-speaker. If you are, there will no doubt be some information about your talk that's communicated in advance of your presentation to members of your audience.

It's crucial to find out exactly what they've been told about your presentation, ahead of time. Word for word. For example, if it's via an e-mail, make sure that you get a copy of it.

I was "burned" a number of times early in my career because I didn't pay enough attention to this. I would develop and present a speech based on an agreement, over the phone, between myself and a representative of the group who had invited me to give a presentation. I would often follow up, via e-mail, with a summary of the agreed-to content and theme of the presentation to the representative. This is an important tip!

Unfortunately, although well intentioned, these representatives often "doctored" this summary, taking artistic license to make the wording more appealing (in their view)in their promotional materials. Unaware of this, I would deliver the agreed-to speech, only to find out afterwards that I hadn't met the group's expectations.

The lesson? Find out exactly what the audience members have been told. Then, and only then can you feel absolutely confident that your presentation's content will be targeted to meet the audience's expectations. And please, if you're the person who's crafted and distributed the pre-presentation information, ensure that you deliver the content as you've described it in the promotional materials.

Don't ever, ever entertain making the fatal mistake of changing the presentation's focus without informing the audience ahead of time.

### Bring On The Questions

If you're conducting a business-oriented presentation, you can usually expect to get some questions coming your way. Take a few minutes after you've developed your content to think about the type of questions you're likely to generate. Then, prepare in your mind the responses to these questions. This will really boost your confidence and your ability to handle the questions.

**Tip:** This is also a fantastic way to buffer your presentation if you have misjudged the timing and it is way too short vs the audience's expectations. Have some pre-defined questions on hand that you can pose rhetorically to the audience and then answer yourself. Or, if it is appropriate, ask these questions directly to your audience.

### Engage For A Win-Win

One of the sure-fire ways of overcoming boredom in any audience is to engage with them during your presentation. Get them actively involved with your ideas. Get them really thinking about your message.

How can you involve your audience? Here are some tips that will help you to involve any audience, any size, anywhere.

**Call Them By Name**

Insert, in your presentation content, the name of a person in your audience or the name of the group your presenting to. This instantly punches through the *invisible barrier* that separates you from your audience. It says, "Hey, wake up. I'm really talking to you! You are special and this isn't just a canned presentation."

**Get A "Show Of Hands"**

Think of a question that requires a "yes" or "no" response. Then, reach out to your audience and request a "show of hands." For example, "How many of you feel...?" Then, acknowledge and deal with both sides of the response as you weave their response into the substance of your presentation.

**Ask For A Volunteer**

Ask for a volunteer to step forward to assist you with something. The rest of the audience will immediately identify with this individual. Be careful that you don't embarrass the volunteer. Make sure it ends up being a positive experience for them.

An example would be getting someone to help you to demonstrate just how easy it is to use a specific product or item. Here's a tip. You'll probably have a better chance of actually getting a volunteer if you don't use the word volunteer. Instead, ask for someone to come up to the front to *assist you* with something. That's how magicians work their magic!

**Question & Answer Session**

This is a great way of getting your audience involved. It will help to create a very natural, conversational tone within your presentation. What if you can't answer a question? These and other challenging situations will be addressed later in this book. However, don't shy away from working a Q&A Session into your presentation where appropriate.

**Get Cozy!**

A really powerful way to break into the audience's "space" is to talk to, or ask questions of, specific individuals in your audience. If you have a large audience in front of you, you can "work with" the people in the front few rows. Everyone will identify with them. For example, think of one of your favorite comedians. They often use this technique to get some folks in the front row of an audience to have some fun and interact with them. It works!

**And finally...**

In this Chapter we've discussed many techniques that you can use to meet the needs of your audience and deal with the presenter's nervousness. The best advice I can offer you in summing up this Chapter is this: Put yourself in your audience's shoes. When you do this, you're thinking like a member of your audience and you'll be right on target. As a matter of fact, you'll probably surprise yourself at just how successful you can be.

How can you project confidence when you honestly don't feel confident? The next Chapter shows you how.

# CHAPTER 3

# FAKE IT 'TIL YOU MAKE IT

"Courage is the art of being the only one who knows you're scared to death."

- Prime Minister of U.K. Harold Wilson (1916-1995)

# IN THIS CHAPTER...

- Using Your Hands Effectively
- Choosing Your Best Moves
- Enjoying Eye Contact
- Employing the Smile Factor
- Discovering your Presenter's Voice

## The Stage Is Yours and You Own It!!

One of the goals most of us aspire to, as presenters, is to appear full of confidence in front of an audience. We've all seen speakers whom we admire who have had a definite air of self-confidence about them. They were in complete control of the situation. They had the audience eating out of the palm of their hands.

How do they do it? Is it a gift, as many people believe? Or can you also learn how to project a confident image?

The good news is that, yes, you can learn how to become a successful, dynamic and confident presenter. There are some specific skills, techniques and mannerisms you can incorporate into all your future presentations to project the confident image that you desire and admire.

This Chapter will show you exactly what you can do to change your style from one that may reflect anxiety and apprehension, to one that exudes confidence. So, take heart my friend and read on.

For many years, I've been fortunate to have had the opportunity to observe the characteristics of thousands of speakers. Speakers on the conference circuit. Speakers involved in service organizations. Speakers doing seminars. Speakers at weddings and social gatherings. And, most important, thousands of speakers participating in my seminars and workshops who wanted to learn presentation techniques.

These participants were the people that taught me the most. They were people just like you who were taking on the challenge of learning how to improve their presentation skills. I had the good fortune of watching them and interviewing them and in that way got in touch with what they felt, and what they needed to do to improve their presentations. I also had the rare opportunity to read and hear the critiques of their colleagues during these workshops, and in that way observe how people in the audience identified effective and confident presenters as opposed to how they identified nervous and much less effective presenters.

**Observations.**

After observing thousands of presenters I've compiled a cornucopia of habits and traits that a confident speaker exhibits versus a stressed and not so confident person. After formulating my "list", I've used it mentally countless times when observing confident speakers and those full of anxiety.

I believe that you will be able to use these techniques to project a confident image for all your future presentations.

**I've Got To Hand It To You**

Let's take a look at the key factors that will reflect either confidence or insecurity *when using your hands.*

An insecure or timid presenter will signal nervousness to an audience by playing unconsciously with his or her hands. If you're nervous, you're likely to:

- Play with objects: pens, markers, paperclips etc.
- Play with the ring or rings on your fingers
- Have your hands hidden during your entire presentation
- Have your arms folded across your chest

If you don't want to look nervous, don't do any of the above.

Here's a few tips that you can use, and you can readily observe in many polished, confident presenters.

## Let 'Em Go!

Use your hands as naturally as possible. If you use them quite a bit in a normal conversation, then use them just as much in your presentations.

Are people always telling you how much you "talk with your hands" when speaking in a conversation? Is it possible to overuse the way you express yourself with your hands? Not usually. If that's how you express yourself, it's your unique personality coming through. Don't be concerned about using your hands in a presentation as often as you do in a natural conversation. Sure, you may use them a lot, but that's part of your "style". Don't hold them back. Think like an Italian!

This last bit of advice flies in the face of many authors on the subject of public speaking. I can imagine they see red when they read this kind of advice. These pundits would suggest that you restrain your hands if you have a tendency to move them around "too much". I, however, couldn't disagree more with this point. Here's why.

First, if you use your hands naturally, they will always compliment what you are saying. That's right, they'll never contradict the words that come out of your mouth. Because of this, your hands can be considered another visual aid. Your hands will visually assist you and your audience in the communication process. They add dynamics to your style, and another dimension to your endeavors to "tell them" your message.

## Don't Do The Right Thing!

Second, if you try to restrain your hands, you'll find that it's so unnatural that it will start to impact (in a negative way) the rest of your style. You'll be far too conscious of your hands, and, in an effort to control their movement you may tend to become too rigid. This will appear to be so unnatural and awkward that your audience will sense that something's amiss. I've seen this happen to hundreds of people in my workshops who are restraining their hand movements in an effort to do the "right thing".

And, finally, remember that your style and personality are unique. It's what makes you special and different from everyone else on earth! So, don't try to strip away that uniqueness or you may end up with a very "bland" image.

**Get Out The Handcuff Key**

Now let's look at the opposite situation i.e., the person who doesn't use their hands much at all. Are you the kind of person who doesn't use your hands in a normal conversation?

There are a number of things that you can do with your hands that will look very natural to your audience. And, here's your key to success. Don't even think about attempting to "talk with your hands" if you don't normally. Why? Because, it will come across as phony and mechanical. And, sensing this, you'll start to be even more self-conscious of your hands. Here are some ideas that will get your hands doing something, without looking awkward.

- If you're using a visual aid, such as an image on a screen, gesture towards the ideas that you are discussing. For example, each time you address a new point, gesture with an open hand to the point on the screen. It directs the audience's attention to a particular point you're discussing, or about to discuss.
- Describe something with your hands. For example, you might be able to indicate the shape of something with your hands. Or, you might show the size of an object by showing its relative

height or width (like the biggest fish you almost caught)! These movements can actually be planned out in advance, and you can prompt yourself to use them from your written notes. Remember, these hand movements will still seem very appropriate and natural to your audience.

- Try emphasizing something with a raised finger. This is a great attention getter and is a super technique to make sure a key point is highlighted for your audience.
- You can also count out your ideas on your fingers. For example, you could say, "First, you should...". Then for the next point, you hold up two fingers and say, "Second...". Once again, these movements can be planned ahead and noted in your notes.

Now, this all sounds so very easy, but just what are you going to do with your hands the other 90% of the time? Fair question! Let's take a look at the "neutral" hand positions.

### When Presenting In Person

What follows are some ideas related to "in person" presentations rather than virtual. Some of these ideas may be valuable if you are being recorded for a promotional presentation for example. I wanted to share these ideas with you for those moments.

### A Hand In Your Pocket Is Not Taboo!

One of the ideas that I suggest people adapt is to put a hand in their pocket when they're not gesturing.

You should realize, however, that putting your hand in your pocket is considered taboo by just about every book ever written on public speaking. If you observe the real world however, you'll observe that many, many confident speakers put their hands in their pockets on occasion, and that includes politicians, actors, CEOs of major corporations and many other high profile people.

Why do some authors and trainers recommend against this? They suggest that it looks sloppy. I disagree. In fact, I think it looks more casual, relaxed and informal than sloppy. And that's not so bad. In fact, most people I have talked to about this believe that it really makes the speaker appear extremely confident.

However, don't get me wrong. I don't believe that you should have one or both hands in your pockets throughout your entire presentation. Remember, variety is the key when thinking about how to use your hands most effectively. But, when you're not gesturing with your hands, or describing things with them, it seems very natural to slip one hand in a pocket, and hold the other one along your side, bent at the elbow so it's parallel to the floor.

Try this pose in front of a mirror and see just how comfortable it looks and feels.

**Don't Get All Bent Out Of Shape**

Here are more tips on some other natural hand positions that you can put in your kit bag when presenting on a live stage:

- Hands occasionally clasped in front of you, either with your arms straight down or bent at the elbow
- Hands behind your back
- Both arms bent at the elbow with your hands in front of your waist
- One arm down at your side, with the other arm bent at the elbow and your hand in front of your waist, at your bellybutton.

As you can see, there really are an endless number of neutral positions for your hands to be in when you're not using them. Ensure that you mix up your hand positions so that a pattern doesn't develop related to where you put your hands when they're not being used. Remember, variety is the key.

I'd like also to emphasize that you should try to avoid the neutral position of having both arms straight down at your side. An audience usually perceives this as a sign of nervousness, the very thing that you're trying to avoid.

In a similar vein, there's another position some presenters inadvertently adopt that can leave a very negative impression: they put both hands on their hips. This is often viewed as a very aggressive posture and should be avoided. Please don't get "all bent out of shape" on the placement of your hands but be aware that if your hands are on your hips it will probably have a negative impression with your audience.

Well, there you have it. Hopefully, a few key ideas on what you can do to help yourself to project a more positive image with your hands. Remember, steer away from any nervous or unnatural use of your hands and relax!

Next, we'll take a look at how to take over the stage.

## Shifting Weight

Ok, here's a sure-fire indicator to an audience that you're nervous. Do a slow waltz in front of the audience and shift your body weight from foot to foot.

Picture in your mind a speaker standing at the front of an audience. Now, imagine the presenter's left knee cocked and the right knee straight. What happens in a weight shift is that on a regular basis the weight is reversed. The right knee will become cocked and the left knee will be straight. This will drive an audience crazy!

Stand up right now and give it a try unless you're in a public transit vehicle! You'll see just how distracting it can be to an audience when a speaker does this. A pattern develops. And, once an audience sees a pattern, they become fixated on it.

If you catch yourself doing this, stop it!

## Going Nowhere Fast

Here's another habit that can drive an audience crazy. A speaker who constantly takes one step forward, then, one step back. He/she really doesn't go anywhere. There's just a constant, distracting movement back and forth. It's probably something akin to a guy learning to dance for the first time. You don't start by cruising around the dance floor like a professional dancer. You practice a simple one-step movement for a while before moving on to the next step.

The problem with a nervous speaker is that there's never a next step! It's just the same old "one step forward and back" that's being practiced over and over and over again in front of an audience. Don't keep practicing, you'll drive your audience crazy.

Then, there's the "pacer". The speaker who takes five steps to the right, turns on his heels, and proceeds to take five steps to the left, turns on his heels and repeats the pattern.

For example, using a white-board tends to bring out the "pacer" in people. I really don't know why, but it just does. Maybe it's a flash back to an image of a teacher in school who constantly paced back and forth in front of the class? Maybe we've picked up this bad habit through osmosis by watching these pacing teachers? Maybe, we just want to be running away! I don't think we can know exactly why you might do it, but please don't do it.

**You Own The Runway!**

A number of years ago I learned how to fly and got my private pilot's license. One thing that always stuck with me is what my flight instructor told me about approaching the runway. As you approach a runway to land, you have to ask the tower for "permission to land." Once the tower says you are "cleared to land", you own the runway. Unless someone declares an emergency, it's all yours baby. You had better get the message, understand it completely and take charge. The tower expects it, your passengers expect it and you better realize in your heart and mind that you are in charge.

So it is with giving a presentation. You own the stage. Your audience knows it and you had better face up to it, acknowledge it and get a grip. It's all yours!

This is an attitude you need to create in your mind whether it's a spotlight that turns on you in a virtual presentation, or when you are on a live stage.

However, I do want to share with you some ideas that you may need if/when you are presenting in front of a live audience.

# THE STAGE IS YOURS

One of the ways that you can demonstrate that you are in control of the stage is to be aware of the movements that indicate this to your audience. So, what exactly should you do as far as movements are concerned? How can you use movement to your advantage, and project an "I own the runway" image?

First, start your presentation standing still. Plant your feet firmly on the ground and do not shuffle around. Don't do any weight shifts, in fact, don't move your feet at all.

Then, and here's the "trick", move with purpose. That's right, move around the front of the room/stage with a specific direction and purpose in mind. How do you do that effectively? Try, for example, taking a couple of steps to the left or right of where you first start your speech. Then, stop. Plant your feet again and don't move them.

After a while, take a few more steps back towards where you started. Plant your feet. Stay there for a while and continue talking. Next, head off to the right or left and continue the process.

Don't forget to mix it up a bit though. Make sure it doesn't look like you're pacing. Or, worse still, you're just rambling about aimlessly at the front of the room. For example, vary the number of paces you move to the left and right of center. Also, vary the timing between your movements.

What I'm really suggesting is that you take charge of the floor. It's your space. You own it! So demonstrate your confidence and take a take charge attitude by walking around, with purpose.

## The Podium

If you have a "podium" or lectern in front of you, you can still move around. Your movements, however, will be somewhat restricted if you are using a microphone.

You can, however, have variety in your body position by turning to face one side of your audience ... moving your feet and body to that side of the audience as you face them. Then, turn and face the center of your audience, squaring up your feet and body to face them directly. Following this, use the same actions for the other side. Once you become comfortable using this technique, you'll discover it's quite simple and looks very natural and confident.

Don't shy away from picking up your microphone (if it's possible), along with a page from your notes and moving around the floor. Some very successful and dynamic speakers capitalize on this technique which shows real flair.

In essence, make your movements direct and forceful. Take charge of the floor, you're "cleared to land!"

## Eye Contact

One of the most powerful skills you can learn to develop is what is commonly referred to as eye contact. It is so important, that I can't stress enough what an essential skill this is.

This is *absolutely crucial* when presenting virtually. Every movement of your eyes is amplified because the camera is directly on your face. And, it is usually a close up of your face and eyes unless it is a group shot in a meeting room.

Do not look down when you're speaking. Do not look up when you're speaking. Do not look at the walls when you're speaking. Do not look out the window when you're speaking.
But, do look directly at the camera whether it is in your laptop/ computer or separate.

This is somewhat difficult for some people because they quite often have a hard time looking people in the eye in informal conversations. If you're one of these types, you'll really have to try very hard to force yourself to overcome this and look directly at the people in your virtual audience. Get over it!

This is something that changes when you may be using a teleprompter. For example, watch when the President of the United States is giving a speech. He (or hopefully she) has three teleprompters... one directly in front, one to the left, and one to the right. This enables them to keep reading their lines on the teleprompter while seemingly looking at members of the audience from left to front to right.

Whatever you do, don't look like a wimp when you're presenting. The last thing you want is for people to feel sorry for you. Why? Because they just plain don't want to feel sorry for you. They want you to look confident because that's what makes them feel comfortable. Then, they can focus on your message, not on you. Using eye contact is the number one way you can project a strong, confident image to your audience. Look them square in the eye through the camera in your laptop!

### Show Us Your Smile!

Each and every one of us is born with the innate ability and instinct to smile. Yet, all too often, speakers wear such a somber look on their faces that you'd swear that every speech they give was somehow connected with a funeral. Hey, lighten up, and at least turn it into an Irish wake(:

A smile is one of your "best bets" for gaining acceptance by, and developing a rapport with, an audience. Why? Because it lets the people in your audience know that you're excited about speaking to them. It lets them know that it is indeed a pleasure for you to be in their company. Plus, it lets them know that you're confident. That, my friend, is a big plus!

Take a look at a confident speaker and watch the expression on his or her face. Chances are that the speaker works in a big smile now and then to reflect a positive attitude. Deliberately working in the "smile factor" reflects a very positive and natural expression. And it is often very calculated.

A smile is quite often also equated with enthusiasm. It demonstrates to your audience that you're really and truly excited about whatever it is that you're telling them.

Remember, you should be the most excited person in the room as it relates to your presentation. If you're not, you'll never "sell" your ideas or get your audience enthused. Even if you tell your audience that you're really excited about your message, but your smile isn't there, your audience many not believe you.

Many presenters tell me that they are so "scared stiff" when they're presenting that they find it extremely hard to smile. They've told me that they don't have anything in their presentation that prompts them to smile. When I've looked over their scripts, I have found that they are usually right. There is nothing there that would encourage a smile. The answer? Write something into your content/material that will allow you to generate a smile in a natural way.

Simply put, try to weave something into your notes (connected to your topic) that will naturally generate a smile on your face. It could be a humorous story or something witty. It could also be a quote from a famous person that could bring a smile to your face and to the faces of the people in your audience. Conversely, you could tell a "horror story" relating something dramatic that happened to you that would bring a smile to your face.

In fact, telling a story as part of your presentation is an extremely effective way to connect with an audience and bring in a smile factor. Some folks say that a well-presented story is one of the most memorable parts of any presentation. I would encourage you to build in a story for ALL your presentations to help build your confidence.

Remember, what you're trying to do is to build something "light" into your presentation that will allow you to work in a natural smile. As mentioned, I call it the "smile factor." I usually review my notes and visual aids with a critical eye and look for the smile factors. If I don't find some, I'll work in an anecdote, or a humorous thought or story that will prompt me to smile naturally during my delivery.

This does not imply that you have to be grinning like a Cheshire cat when you're giving a speech, constantly beaming from ear to ear. Just work in a smile now and then to show your audience a positive and pleasing side of your personality. Show them that you really are enjoying the pleasure of their company.

### Be Expressive

I read something that a cynical presenter said in a joking way "Once you can fake sincerity, you've got it made!" Yes, you can fake a lot of things. Unfortunately, I don't believe that you can fake sincerity in front of an audience. You can fool yourself into thinking that you're fooling your audience, but their instincts will let them know you're not sincere. So, be genuine, find something to get truly excited about, and express it.

Remember, we judge ourselves by our feelings. On the other hand, people in our audiences judge us by our actions.

For example, imagine you start off your speech by saying, "Good morning ladies and gentlemen. It's a pleasure to be here today to talk to you about something that I find very exciting."

Your words are telling your audience how you feel about being there. You are extremely pleased to be in their company. However, if you present these opening comments with a very somber look on your face, your audience simply won't believe you. There will be a conflict in their minds between the words you speak, and what's reflected in your facial expression and overall body language. And, believe me, they'll intuitively judge you by how you look, rather than the words you choose to express yourself...every time!

I'm sorry to say that this perception is truly a shame. Why? Because you may be indeed be very genuinely excited about what it is you have to say to them. However, they'll never believe you if you don't say the words with a smile on your face and with genuine enthusiasm in your voice. So, when you're saying something that, in any way, shape or form represents something positive, be sure to let your smile reflect those positive thoughts.

**Speak Up**

All confident speakers, yes all of them, have one trait in common. You can "hear" the confidence in their voices. How can you emulate this so that you too can project confidence via your voice. First, and foremost, simply speak up! That's right. Speak up. Project your voice. Raise the volume level of your voice so that you are speaking with conviction.

I have three words at the top of every set of Notes that I use. They are "up and loud." The "up" relates to psyching myself up for the presentation (as discussed earlier). The "loud" reminds me to raise my voice so that those farthest away from me have absolutely no difficulty in hearing my words. Of course, in a virtual presentation this is much easier since your mic should be able to pick up your voice and people can adjust their volume. However, both of these words still come into play as they relate to being a confidence booster.

The level of volume used sets apart the confident presenter from the timid one. If you want to project confidence and a positive image, then you must use a strong and firm voice. No doubt you've seen movies of an army drill instructor putting the green recruits through their paces. Was he confident? Did he project confidence? You bet he did! How could you tell? By his voice. And, by-and-large, by the volume and intensity of his voice. And often by the stream of profanity that is directed at some poor, quivering recruit(:

Now, don't get me wrong, I'm not suggesting that you should sound and act like a drill instructor when you deliver your speech. However, it is a fact that people often equate a speaker's confidence level with their voice level.

Ideally, I'd recommend that you try to speak with conviction. Let your audience hear your message loud and clear.

Many presenters that I've coached, who are soft spoken by nature, have a great deal of difficulty in raising their voices. They feel very awkward when they speak up. They feel that they are being "phony," that it really "isn't them".

However, it's important when they realized that raising their volume is not artificial or phony at all. Everyone is capable of raising his or her voice. Witness people when they get angry! It's demonstrable proof that volume is a dimension of a person's voice that can be manipulated so that an audience can hear the speaker. Speak up, it's okay. It conveys confidence.

### Don't Shout

What volume level should you speak at if you're not equipped with a microphone? Ideally, it will be at a level that the person farthest away from you in the room won't have to strain to hear you. They should be able to sit back and relax, and not be concerned about your volume level.

So the key person to target in the room is (you guessed it) the person sitting farthest from the front. You have to look right at that individual and talk directly to him/her. It's important to look directly at that person so that in your mind's eye you really do see the distance between you and that person. A glance in their direction won't do. You need a concrete reference point in order to adjust your volume to the right level.

### How Loud Is Loud?

You can practice various volume levels by having a colleague sit at the very back of a presentation room. Start off standing close to this person and reciting something. Anything will do. Now, as you keep repeating reciting, start to back up, gradually getting farther away. And, as you retreat towards the front of the room, raise your voice.

Ask your colleague to let you know if it's too low to hear you comfortably. When you've reached the farthest distance that the room permits, make a mental note of the volume level that you are speaking at. Really listen to the volume at which you are speaking and fix that level firmly in your mind for future reference.

Now, slowly start to reverse the procedure and walk closer to your colleague. As you do this, lower your volume ... being sensitive to the comfort level that's ideal for that person to listen to. Once again, if it's too loud or soft, ask them to tell you to raise or lower your voice.

After going through this process a few times, you'll quickly ascertain how much you will need to adjust the volume of your voice. Remember, ideally your voice should be at a level that anyone can comfortably listen to, regardless of where in the room they're sitting. You can be very confident that if the person farthest away from you in the room is able to hear you, then everyone else between you and that person can also hear you.

## Variety Is The Spice Of Life

Like life, the ups and downs in your voice pattern will add interest to your presentation. Varying the inflection and intensity in your voice is also an important skill that you can develop and cultivate that will project confidence. If your voice tone is flat and uninteresting, your audience will be uninterested in what you have to say. Your voice will lack the confidence to catch and hold their interest in your message.

What can you do to be more captivating? Add variety in your voice. For example, you can underscore and highlight some key points in your speech by saying them with much more vigor. Put flavor and excitement in your voice. Speak with passion!

It seems that many of us have lost touch with the natural richness that we all have in our voices. To rediscover these underused qualities, read a passage from a book out loud. Select a page which has an exciting event taking place. Read it aloud, placing exaggerated emphasis on the words. You'll be amazed and delighted with just how much inflection and quality you still have in your voice. Get in touch with it again and try to transfer it to your speech making endeavors.

### What You See Is What They Get

Add zest to your presentation by including some snappy sentences, quotations or points. This will provide you with an opportunity to add the inflection that enriches your presentation. Underline some key words to remind you to add intensity and variety with your voice. I can assure you that most professional narrators "mark up" their scripts in a similar fashion. Or, if in a virtual presentation, underline a key point on a visual to prompt you to add some inflection.

Your voice is yet another crucial link in projecting a positive, confident image. If you find yourself wondering what you can do to help yourself feel more confident, speak up and use variety.

### They Love Me...They Love Me Not

During my "how to" seminars on presentation techniques I demonstrated to participants how they can project confidence and get the audience "loving" them. First, I showed them the difference between a confident speaker and one who gives the "appearance" of being confident.

Each speaker I portrayed used exactly the same words, so the content was the same. The only variable was the manner in which it was delivered. I demonstrate both the non-confident and confident speaker by getting up at the front of the participants and saying... "Good morning ladies and gentlemen. It's a real pleasure to be here today to talk to you about an exciting, new employee benefit program."

The first time I delivered it I said the words very flat with no inflection. The second time I added some ZIP!!

There is a dramatic difference between the two approaches to speaking. The unconfident speaker is seen as insecure and extremely anxious. The other speaker is judged as being very confident, a person who is sincerely excited about what he's about to present.

It's important to note that the speaker (me) was the same in both cases. The words spoken are exactly the same. Yet, the perception of one speaker's level of confidence over the other is quite remarkable. What's the difference? Read on.

## The Nervous Presenter's Behaviors

After the demonstration I asked the group to identify some key behaviors they observed which indicated to them that **the first speaker was nervous** and apprehensive about the circumstances he found himself in. Here's what they say about the nervous speaker:

- Walked up to the front of the room with short, timid steps.
- Clutched his notes between both hands in a death grip (I call it the "dentist chair" grip).
- Didn't gesture at all.
- Read his notes word for word.
- Had little if any eye contact with his audience.
- Had a somber, worried look on his face.
- Spoke very quietly.
- Didn't smile.

- Cowered over his notes with his head down.
- Stood rigid, and in one spot.

Yikes! That's a painful litany of behaviors that really would not excite any audience anywhere!!

## The Powerful Presenter's Behaviors

The confident, effective speaker exhibited just about the exact opposite behaviors of a timid speaker. Here's what audiences had to say about the confident speaker:

- Walked up to the front of the room with even, sure steps.
- Held his index card notes comfortably and unobtrusively in one hand, while gesturing naturally with the other.
- Glanced at his notes just once, but he didn't read them.
- Looked around at his entire audience.
- Smiled.
- Spoke up.
- Had good posture, but was not "stiff".

## The Perception Was Everything

The difference between the audience's perception of these two speakers is really quite remarkable. The demonstration took less than ten seconds. Yet, the perception of anxiety or confidence is clearly established in the audience's mind by the end of those brief ten seconds. Quite powerful when you think of the short timeframe involved!

And just how did they determine if one speaker was confident and the other speaker wasn't? They mentally noted some of the behaviors exhibited during those short, opening remarks. Behaviors that reflected the presenter's comfort and confidence level.

The good news for you is that you can very deliberately, even mechanically, incorporate some of the behaviors exhibited by the confident speaker into all of your presentations. You can project that confidence in the first ten seconds of every presentation you give, and rest assured that the audience truly believes that you are very confident. If you do this, your audience will quickly relax and be convinced that you are a very polished, self-assured speaker.

Yes, you really can fool them even if you are nervous. Also, because your audience relaxes, you can relax also. They'll never know just how nervous you are if you simply adopt some traits of a confident presenter.

This also holds true for virtual presentations. The way you present yourself during this first 10 secs. Goes a long way to establishing your confidence.

Remember, there's nothing magical about any of this. It is something that you can do for yourself in your very next presentation. It's also something that you can observe for yourself. To prove just how powerful our perception of a person's confidence is, based on observable behaviors, take close note of the speakers that you see in real life, on television, or in a virtual meeting or webinar.

When observing a confident speaker, jot down in point form, a list of behaviors that the speaker is exhibiting, such as smiling, volume of voice and eye contact. If the speaker seems nervous, make notes of the behaviors that trigger this perception. You'll quickly see that there are some readily identifiable traits that we use to judge whether a speaker is nervous or not.

**In Summary**

What you've just finished reading are some extremely effective techniques and skills that you can use to project a much desired and welcomed confident impression.

Your audience really wants you to be confident. They don't want to feel sorry for you. They don't want you to be nervous. Why? Because this makes them feel uneasy. Uncomfortable. Guilty. They want to relax and listen to your message. They can only truly relax if you also appear to be relaxed.

The appearance of being relaxed (even if you're not) is very important. I've used the word "projecting" a confident image throughout this Chapter. If you learn to use these techniques to project confidence, I can assure you that you will start to feel more confident and relaxed.

If you want to look like a confident presenter then work on eliminating those habits and traits that reflect nervousness. Replace them with behaviors that will automatically lead your audience to view you as a very confident presenter.

Remember, act confident and you'll feel confident!

Another way to step up a rung or two on your confidence ladder is to carefully and deliberately plan every stage of your presentation. Design it in such a way that it's foolproof and you're almost assured of success. How can you do this? Read on...

# CHAPTER 4
# YOUR ROADMAP TO SUCCESS

"Live as brave men, and if fortune is adverse,
front its blows with brave hearts."
- Cicero (106 BC-43 BC)

# IN THIS CHAPTER...

- Step-by-step Design
- Motivating Any Audience
- Constructing Your Presentation's Key Ideas
- Wrapping Up Your Presentation With Style

## It's Nothing To Do With Luck

One of the key ingredients for success in any part of our lives is to "plan" for success. However, all too often we rely on Lady Luck to smile down upon us. Sometimes she does, and good fortune comes our way. However, trust me when I say that Lady Luck has no place in preparing for successful presentations. If you really want to be confident, plan your speech. You'll find it to be a tremendous confidence booster. As well, it will definitely give you a much better chance to succeed.

Sailors who challenge the world's vast oceans in dinky little sailboats realize that it is absolutely essential to plan ahead in order for them to succeed and even survive. They must, for example, determine ahead of time what supplies and resources they will need. They must ensure that the necessary navigational equipment/GPS is in good working order (and have a backup sextant just in case). And you can bet they spend many hours charting a course for themselves.

You must also take the time to chart a course for yourself in order to design a winning speech. First, find a quiet secluded spot where you can plan the course of events and points that you'll include in your presentation, points that will be milestones along the way that enable you to get your message across to your audience.

Once you're settled into that quiet space, you'll run smack into one of the most troublesome roadblocks that most presenters face: Where do you start?

## The Beginning

What I'm about to introduce you to is a structure that will show you where to start and get you over any obstacles you have in short order. This is a framework you can use for any speech or presentation you'll be asked to make in your entire life, regardless of the subject matter. Naturally, you can use this framework as a guide and modify it as you see fit. However, it will always work!

You can view this as an approach or a process. And, in much the same way as a sailor charts a course using a series of steps to reach his or her destination, you can in a similar fashion chart your course to success.

**Navigating To Success**

In the days of old sailing ships, mariners used a sextant to assist them in going step-by-step along a planned route. This process of mapping a route and traveling on a given course was a system that they could always rely on even if the body of water changed. It didn't matter if the trip was to the Mediterranean or cruising the Caribbean, the process of laying out a course and ensuring the boat was on track remained the same. Mariners were confident that the tools and techniques they used would hold them in good stead no matter what waters they were traveling on.

You too can use the following system or process for any topic or type of presentation you'll be asked to give in the future. It doesn't matter if it's a speech at a wedding, at a service club, or you're talking in front of a Board Of Directors. It doesn't matter if it is a video call, a webinar, or a ZOOM call. The audience may change, the subject matter may change, but the technique remains constant. This is a proven, very successful way to design a winning presentation.

## It's Love In Italian!

This technique is one that you can easily remember forever. The first letter of each of the steps forms the Italian word for love. Which is? AMORE. So, my friend, all you have to do to remember the steps involved is to think about adding a little "love" into your presentation. Italian love that is!

Let's break down the acronym, AMORE, and look at each of the steps in detail.

## Ready, AIM, Fire

The first letter, "A" in AMORE represents the word *Aim*. This is the very first thing that you should think about when designing any speech. What is the purpose of your presentation?

Take some quality time to think about it very carefully. Make sure that the purpose of your presentation is crystal clear in your own mind. After all, this is the purpose of your entire presentation and it will frame the nature and the scope of the content that you will be developing.

Once you have thought about it, write it down in plain English. Ensure that the words describing your purpose are clear, meaningful and concise.

If you can't write down your aim in one or two sentences, then re-think what your speech is all about. Take your time. Don't rush. Remember that your Aim and the way you articulate it will form the foundation for all of the points in your presentation. It's a no-nonsense statement of intent. As the army describes it when teaching officers presentation techniques: "Tell 'em what you're going to tell 'em."

## For Example?

Here's a look at a few examples of how you can create an Aim.

If you were planning on giving a business presentation outlining the positive attributes of a new computer system being introduced into your office environment, you might say:

"Good morning and welcome. The purpose of my presentation is to introduce you to the features and benefits of our new and improved financial accounting system."

Or, if you were giving a presentation to a service club in your community, you might start by saying:

"Good evening ladies and gentlemen. I'm delighted to be here today to share with you some ideas on how we can successfully raise some funds for our new community swimming pool."

And finally, here's an example of how you can craft an aim if you had the good fortune to be asked to be the best man at a friend's wedding (Wow...can that be painful!):

"Ladies and gentlemen, I'd like to spend a little time with you during this festive occasion to share with you some little-know yet fascinating insights into the groom's shady past!" I think you can just imagine how that "aim" would have everyone riveted to their seats, have their undivided attention and create an air of absolute anticipation! Words matter.

Each of these openings was geared for a different audience. Each opening described a different topic or message. Yet each one very clearly and effectively prepared the audience for the speech that was to follow.

**Keep It Simple**

Here is another really important point related to opening statements. They should be very simple, and very much to the point. There should be no doubt left in the audience's mind related to what the speech is going to focus on. Why? If you don't make your Aim clear and concise at the outset you run the very real risk of losing your audience as soon as you begin. Here's a real-life situation I want to share with you that really drove this point home to me.

I was sitting in a meeting that got off to a very awkward start. The presenter jumped right into the main body of his presentation without stating his purpose. We were catapulted into an in-depth dissertation before we got settled into our chairs. After about ten minutes, a person two rows back from where I was seated gingerly put up his hand and said, "Excuse me, but I think that I'm in the wrong meeting." He then proceeded, red faced, out of the room and left.

Holy cow! It took him a full ten minutes to determine he was in the wrong room. Ten long minutes to figure out what the speaker's message was. Ten minutes to realize what the aim of the presentation was. The speaker had simply failed to tell audience his "Aim".

Do not allow yourself to fall into this trap. Remember that the AIM is the first step in your AMORE formula for success. Not clearly defining your aim can lead to catastrophic results.

The next step in your AMORE sequence is something that is all too often overlooked by many experienced and inexperienced presenters alike. Whatever you do, don't omit this next step in your path to success.

**MOTIVATE!**

The second letter in AMORE stands for *Motivation*. Once you've established your aim with the audience, you have to create interest in your message. Here's where the motivational dimension to your presentation comes into play.

Quite often people in your audience will already be motivated to listen to your message. If they are that's a real bonus! However, if they're not motivated, it is up to you to motivate them. They already may be interested, but they may not know just how truly valuable your presentation ideas might be to them.

Unfortunately, people will sometimes be "sent" to listen to your presentation, especially if it's a business-oriented one. Or they may be just plain apathetic towards your subject matter... or, maybe they are just there for the free lunch (:

So, it's up to you to try to motivate them to listen and absorb. How? Well, I could really spend the remaining pages of this book on the subject of motivating people. And it really is a fascinating subject. However, I think in the context of presentations there are some very key, practical ideas that will allow you to decide for yourself how to best motivate your audience.

Over the years, I've discovered that it usually takes only two or three thought provoking points to motivate people to listen to a presentation. In order to decide what these key points will be, sit back and put yourself in your audience's shoes. Think of what would motivate you, as a member of the audience. Think in particular about your subject matter and decide what BENEFITS you would derive from listening to the topic. What would prompt your audience to listen?

What's With The Foot Odor?

But, you may ask, how can you be sure that what you think will motivate the audience to listen will really work? You can't be one hundred percent sure. And, my friend, that's okay. But, taking an **educated guess at one or more factors that will potentially motivate your audience to listen will probably pay** off most of the time.

Let me give you an example. Let me try an experiment with

you. I'd like you to take a look at the shoes/footwear that you have on your feet right now. If you don't have any on, think of what you were wearing earlier in the day. Now, before you read on (and don't cheat), I'd like you to think of three reasons you bought (or like wearing) those particular shoes. Take a moment right now to reflect on the reasons.

I would hazard a guess that you thought of at least one of the following:

- Color
- Quality
- Looks/Style
- Price

These points may seem rather obvious and natural in enabling me to guess what motivated you to buy those shoes. But that's exactly my point! I was fairly confident in my capability to determine ahead of time the things that motivated you.

If you put yourself in your audience's shoes (pun intended) and remember this experiment, you too can quickly determine the motivational factors that should tweak your audience's interests. All it takes is a wee bit of dedicated thought ahead of time.

**Show Me The Money**

The following list of motivational factors may help you convey some tangible benefits for your future audiences. These are standard benefits that can be directly associated with many topics:

- Reduce some fears/risks?
- Save time?
- Save dollars?

- Make Money?
- Increase productivity?
- Enjoy work more?
- Have more fun!
- Advance your career?
- Beat the competition?
- Do something easier?
- Do something quicker?
- Be more informed?
- Gain new insights?
- Be better prepared?
- Discover new options?

As you can see, there are countless ways that you can motivate an audience. Work in two or three benefits during the opening portion of your presentation. If you do, you can stimulate your audience to listen to your message. And this is going to help you to achieve your goal–to get your message across successfully.

## Pose Questions

One technique you might use to successfully build motivation into your presentations is to pose rhetorical questions. Here's an example:

**AIM:** *"Good morning ladies and gentlemen. It's a pleasure to be here today to introduce you to the latest addition to our product line. It's called the Super Widget!"*

**MOTIVATION:** *"How is it going to help you save time, increase productivity, and beat the competition? I'll tell you how in the next twenty minutes."*

As you can see, you can weave into your presentations a number of motivational factors that will really stimulate your audience. Make them sit up and pay attention. Make them thirst for the information you're about to provide.

Be sure to build motivation into every presentation you conduct. It's just one more important key to a professional and successful presentation.

**The OUTLINE?**

The third letter in AMORE, "O", stands for *Outline.* The outline conveys to your audience the main ideas that you intend to unfold during the course of your presentation.

What ideas are you going to unfold? What order should these points be in? How much information should you include under each main idea before moving on to the next? Let's take a look at these and other factors that can result in developing a successful Outline.

**Brainwriting Your Way To Success**

The first thing you should do, when trying to decide what main points to include in your *Outline,* is to look closely at your Aim. Think very carefully about the main message of your presentation and then start writing down some key ideas that will contribute towards your Aim. What are the main ideas that you want to bring out to support your main message.

Start to list your ideas as freely as you can (I call this brainwriting!). Keep within the scope of your aim, but let your mind throw out ideas. In essence, you're not really making any judgments on the ideas you're putting down at this time, but you're letting your thoughts run free. In this way, you have a better chance of thinking of some ideas that might be overlooked if you started to pre-judge them.

## What Prompts You?

One way of prompting your mind to come up with ideas that are relevant to your topic is to use the following technique.

Answer these questions and relate them to the main ideas that are important for the audience to know.

- Who?
- Where?
- What?
- How?
- When?
- Why?

Try to think of five or six main ideas that you want to get across to support your Aim. Add supporting details to these main ideas to make the message around each point crystal clear in the minds of your audience. Organize these five or six points in order of importance.

## Getting Organized

Quite often your ideas can be organized very quickly. A natural relationship often exists between the ideas, and one idea will quite naturally be presented before another.

For example, if your speech was about "How To Fly An Airplane," you might describe the principles of flight, followed by a description of the function of the various parts of the plane, and follow this up by describing how to operate the controls. This, as you can see, would be a very natural and orderly way of organizing your ideas.

In other presentations it can be more difficult to figure out how to put it all together. Sometimes, there just doesn't seem to be any real compelling reason to put one particular point in your outline ahead of another. Each point can stand by itself and it contributes in a very independent way towards the Aim.

For example, imagine that you were designing a presentation to enlighten people on the various forms of pollution in the area where they live. You could discuss the various types of air, water and noise pollution. Each point contributes to the topic equally, they're not really dependent on each other, and the order of these points is of little consequence.

Here are a couple of other key things to remember when developing an outline:

- Always ensure your points connect back to your Aim. Do they cover the subject thoroughly? Will they keep your presentation on track?
- Always ensure that the benefits to your audience (that you described in your Motivation) will be addressed under the topics in your outline. Remember, you have set some expectations and your audience expects you to deliver!
- Ensure your Outline is one that gives the impression of clarity, continuity and organization.

Your Outline is a skeletal framework for your speech. It is the backbone of your entire presentation. Put a lot of thought into it. Ensure that all the essential ideas will be addressed.

Once you've decided on your Outline, your next step is to flesh it out and add some details around each of your main ideas. Let's take a close look at how you can develop the details of your presentation. We call this the body.

## The Main Body

Each of the points in your Outline should combine to support your Aim. They are, essentially, the key ideas that you want to convey to your audience.

Now is the time to add some supporting details around each

of your points. These supporting details are called sub-ideas, or sub-points. They describe your key ideas in more detail.

This is, quite frankly, the easiest part of developing any presentation. Why? Because all you have to do is focus on one main point (identified in your outline) at a time, and then expand on that idea, and that idea alone.

How much detail should you weave around each point? Well, that really depends on how much time you have for your presentation. And how much information it takes to make your point perfectly clear in the minds of the people in your audience.

A rule of thumb is to have no more than five or six sub-points around each main point. Your audience is only capable of keeping that many points connected to one major point. More than that and you run the very real risk of your audience getting lost in all of the detail. Their eyes will glass over and they will tend to drift off.

So, just what sub-points should you include in your presentation to "flesh it out"? The answer...is whatever you feel will help your audience to grasp the idea that you're trying to get across in a succinct way.

## Let's Look At It Step-By-Step

Let's pause for a moment and put everything we've covered into perspective.

You've determined the Aim of your presentation. Next, you've put together the benefits that your audience will derive from listening to your presentation i.e. you've built in the Motivation. Your Outline came next. It formed the framework indicating the main points you want to convey.

Each of the points in your Outline was then expanded by creating some sub-points. You're actually building up your entire presentation in a modular fashion. Each of the points in your Outline is really a module that is part of the whole. We're looking at a holistic approach.

Using this technique, you can see that a presentation really consists of an Aim that is divided into modules, and each module is further sub-divided into supporting details.

This method can be used to develop any presentation. Simply take a large idea and MODULARIZE IT.

### The Digestive System

Your audience effectively "digests" ideas that are presented in small, palatable packages or "modules". By presenting these ideas in modules, your audience will be better able to organize your thoughts in their heads.

Once your major modules and supporting points are organized you've developed the main "body" of your presentation. Now, there is one major consideration that you need to consider at this time. You have to link your modules together so that they "flow" as a unified whole.

What does that mean? Well, have you ever been to a presentation where the facts were well presented, but the presentation seemed "choppy"? Did it seem like the presenter was presenting one idea after another as if reading from a shopping list? If so, the problem was that the presenter didn't join or link the modules together to make his presentation flow smoothly. Oh, all the relevant details were there all right, but, it just didn't seem to be anything but a presentation of non-connected, independent points.

If the presenter had only joined his or her major points with "links", it would have been far more effective. Much easier to listen to and much more "professional."

These links, which connect one module to the next, are called "transitional links". I call it joining the dots. They are, in fact, words that you can use to introduce the next main point that you are going to delve into. It is often called a segue.

Here are a few typical examples of transitional links that you can consider using in a presentation:

- "Next, let's take a look at..."
- "But, how will it work? That's what we'll examine next."
- "Step three is..."
- "We've looked at how it will work. But how much is this going to cost? Let's now take a look at the related expenses."
- "Another fascinating aspect which we'll explore right now is..."

Get the idea? These statements or questions lead your audience into your next train of thought. They introduce your next major topic. They form a transition, or bridge, across your major ideas.

**Why Is This So Important?**

Links are very important! First and foremost, they prepare your listeners' minds for the change of thought that's about to take place. It smoothly "eases" them into the next major point you're about to make. It is, in effect, the thread that links or joins all the ideas into one unit. You simply keep connecting the dots, showing the "thread" that strings one idea to the next.

Plus, it ensures that your presentation flows ever so smoothly. What does this mean? It means that your audience will find it that much easier to listen to your ideas. Not only are your ideas logically connected by this "transitional link", but they're also audibly connected as well. There won't be those awkward, embarrassing, silent gaps between points. These gaps (of inordinately lengthy silence) are as disconcerting to the audience as they are to you.

So, to avoid this problem simply introduce your next main idea. Then, you can comfortably pause to gather your thoughts. The pause is natural enough that people automatically realize that it's time to adjust to a new set of ideas.

## The Missing Link

The key to designing a truly successful presentation that gets your ideas/message across is to think carefully about what your audience needs to know in order to understand your message. Then, simply modularize your information and link the modules together. If you view the task of designing a presentation as simply developing and organizing modules, you'll have taken a giant step towards successfully getting your points across.

There's also a bonus in store for you if you use this method to design your winning presentation. You'll never have to feel anxious about being asked to prepare and present a somewhat longer presentation. Why? Because if you modularize your presentation, it's simply a matter of adding additional, or lengthier modules to your presentation to meet the time goals. A one-hour presentation seems overwhelming, but by modularizing your presentation you only have six ten-minute modules.

Next? It's time to recap your presentation.

## Cap It With A RECAP

The letter "R" in AMORE represents the *Recap*. To recap is to summarize your main ideas. Once you've delivered your main message and covered all the bases in your presentation, it's time to recap.

The recap is an essential ingredient in our AMORE technique. It re-focuses your audience on the main substance of your topic.

You've covered a lot of ground during your presentation. Many different issues, concepts or facts may have been discussed. Quite often some ideas may have been expanded on that weren't entirely crucial or germane to the understanding of your main message. Or, additional ideas may have contributed to the topic at hand. The recap provides a presenter with an opportunity to put some order to what has transpired. To identify, once again, the main ideas that you want your audience to remember about your message.

Your audience may also have voiced disagreement with some aspects of your presentation or challenged your ideas. This interaction often takes some time to resolve during the course of your presentation, even though it is usually very healthy and fruitful.

A recap gives you the opportunity to leverage the results of this dialogue and gives you the ideal opportunity to assist you in driving your message home. It will allow you to accentuate the positive and to reinforce the important points that may have been overshadowed by some distractions during the course of your presentation.

**Let Us Out Of Here... Please!**

What should you recap? Only your main points. Do not fall into the trap of going over many of the detailed points that were covered. This will be perceived as redundant and a waste of time and you will turn your audience off. Towards the end of your presentation, you and your audience want to get out of there!

Be selective about what you decide to recap – the points that formed the substance of your message. Many presenters simply restate the main points from their Outline. This is an effective and natural technique. It also sends a strong message out to your audience – here's what I said we'd cover in the presentation and I did. You kept your "contract" with them.

However, sometimes it's wise if you recap or summarize at times other than at the conclusion of your presentation. When would this be effective? It can often be used effectively if you have:

- just presented a detailed or complex module
- had a rather lengthy module to present
- engaged in a "heated" discussion and a summary of the salient points would be beneficial

Here are a few examples of what a recap might sound like in your presentation:

- *"Ladies and gentlemen, we've looked at five ways in which we can improve our sales in this quarter and take on the competition. They are..."*
- *"I'd just like to summarize some of the key points that we've explored together this afternoon. First.."*
- *"During this presentation we've seen that it's important to..."*

Recapping is an integral part of the AMORE technique. It's a way of demonstrating to your audience that something tangible and positive has been accomplished. And, of equal importance, it's a way of helping them to remember the key ideas connected to your message.

The letter "E" in AMORE? It stands for the *Ending* of your presentation. Let's turn our attention to some crucial considerations when you're into the final stage of your speech.

**The "Grand Finally"**

The ending of your presentation can make or break your entire presentation!

This fact is all too often overlooked when people design and develop their presentations. For example, you may have put so much time and personal energy into creating the main "guts" of your presentation that when it comes time to designing your ending you may not have any creative energy or patience left!

What I think happens is that when you've finally crafted the body of your presentation it becomes a psychological "end point." You have a feeling of completion and accomplishment. You have a strong sense that the message that you have so carefully crafted will be successfully communicated, and at long last the dog work is finally over! All that's left is to "finish it off" with a brief recap and ending. No sweat!

Unfortunately, your Ending will not come quite as naturally and easily as your Recap. Your Recap is a little easier to develop because it basically restates your points in your Outline. It's not so easy, my friend, with your closing remarks.

The words that you choose to close off your speech should be chosen very, very carefully AND ahead of time. You should avoid AT ALL COSTS trying to conjure up closing remarks during the final remaining moments of your speech. You have just too much at stake.

Too much can go wrong. You've invested too much into this important presentation. Remember, your final words of expression will leave a lasting impression! Let's take a closer look.

### Parting Is Such Sweet Sorrow

Your ending offers you a huge opportunity, an opportunity to leave a memorable idea about your message in the minds of your audience. A time when you can inject some poignant remarks that will be forever fixed in their minds.

To do this effectively, it will take careful planning and forethought on your part. Do not shortchange yourself! Put in that extra 10% of time and energy to really make your ending one of the most memorable parts of your entire presentation.

Don't forget, every single person in your audience always perks up and listens when they hear those telling words: "And in closing, I'd just like to say..." It's nothing personal, but some people may even say...thank God! Especially, if it has been a long speech. So, take advantage of their alertness to leave them with a positive and lasting impression.

**Go Ahead...Make Their Day!**

How can you close off your presentation with panache? Here are just a few ideas that might give you some direction when you're choosing your own closing remarks.

Compliment your audience. That's right... flatter them. Tell them how great they've been. Tell them that, in fact, they have been "*just a fantastic audience.*"

Tell them how much you have appreciated their:

- Interest
- Feedback
- Attention
- Questions
- Dialogue
- Participation etc.

If appropriate, *encourage* them to try to put your ideas into practice. In fact, it's very powerful if you use the word "encourage". It's a powerful word because it indicates very clearly you believe in the value of what you've presented and tells them in no uncertain terms that you have faith that your ideas will work for them if they implement them. Simply say something such as *"I'd like to encourage you to ..."* And, then finish this off with a few ideas that you'd like them to try based on your speech. Or simply encourage them to "think" about incorporating some of your ideas in the near future.

*Challenge* them. Yes, throw out a very clear challenge to your audience to try and incorporate your ideas. People respond to a challenge to accomplish something, to meet new goals for themselves. For example, say *"I'd like to challenge each of you to..."*.

*Support* them. Indicate to your audience the type of support they can receive from you when implementing your ideas. It may not be in the form of direct support from you, but it might come from your department or company etc. It leaves them with a very positive feeling to know that you're truly interested in them as individuals, that you will be as supportive as you possibly can.

A very effective idea I've seen used in many successful presentations is to leave your audience members with a telephone number or e-mail address. It really demonstrates that you have a personal commitment to them if they need your assistance or want to talk something over in the future.

*Thank* them. This is something that is sometimes discouraged by people who wrongly feel that a "thank you" to your audience has no place in a presentation. They say that it sounds shallow and insincere. That your audience doesn't need to be thanked because you're the one who has given something of value to them. They say, that it's your audience that they should be thanking you.

I think that's wrong. Your audience has given part of their day to listen to you. They have given part of their life to you.

Hey...the least you can do is thank them for their time, attention, and consideration of your ideas!

I'll quite often say "Thank you for the privilege of your time." as the very last words in my presentation. Why? Because in addition to the reasons I've already discussed, it also indicates to my audience that my presentation has reached a conclusion. It's over! There is absolutely no doubt in the audience's mind when I smile, bow my head, and say those words. It is the finale.

**It's Over...The Band Has Left The Building!**

These then, are just some ideas that you can incorporate into your own "closing". Use your imagination and craft your own words to bring your presentation to a positive and polished conclusion.

Think about the words you'll use ahead of time. You might find it effective if you set aside some quality time after you've developed the body of your presentation and your recap. Set aside some time, after you've had a break from developing the main part of your presentation. Then think about your ending and the words you'll choose to close off your presentation. It will give you an opportunity to compose your ending with a fresh and relaxed mind. And it will ensure that you're not rushing the creative process of choosing the words you will use for your ending.

Your ending is an extremely important aspect of your presentation. Underestimating its impact and not being prepared for the ending can result in your presentation simply "fizzling out" at the end. Giving your closing remarks the time and attention they deserve can pay huge dividends when you actually deliver them.

So, there you have it. A plan you can use to structure any kind of presentation you're called upon to give. The topic doesn't really matter. Just use the AMORE structure and you'll find your development efforts will unfold easily, naturally and quickly.

Why is this planning so important? Because having a plan gives you immediate focus. It provides a framework that allows you to concentrate more on content than on structure. And it ensures that you're developing your ideas in a proven manner that will lead to a smooth and logical delivery.

In many ways, it also helps you to gain more confidence. If you know you're doing it "right" you will present your ideas with more with confidence. You know that whatever else may happen to impact your delivery in a negative way, this structure will still be successful. It will also provide your audience with a clearly defined structure that they can use to follow your ideas and facilitate the communication process.

My final message to you...stick to the AMORE plan. Apply it. Let your confidence level soar because you can be assured that you're using a "tried and true" method!

Next, you're going to discover some dynamite techniques for designing and delivering visuals that will assist you in building your confidence even more.

# CHAPTER 5

# VISUALIZE IT!

"Whatever you can do or dream you can, begin it.
Boldness has genius, power and magic in it."

- Johann Wolfgang von Goethe (1794 – 1832)

# IN THIS CHAPTER...

- The power of visual aids
- Choosing the most powerful aids
- Using visuals effectively
- Pros and Cons of the most common visuals

## Aid Yourself

Visual aids help both you and your audience. In this chapter we'll delve into some of the more common, and not so common, visual aids that you can use to add an exciting dimension to many of your presentations.

First, let's take a look at how visuals can help you to become a more confident presenter.

One of the most unsettling things that can happen during a presentation is that everyone in the audience focuses their attention on you. You become the feature attraction. You become the focal point that rivets their attention. This thought may make you feel very uncomfortable. What can you do to get out of this situation?

Often, the most uncomfortable moment for most presenters is at the very beginning of a presentation. The idle chatter swiftly fades when you go to the front of the room. The crowd becomes silent and all eyes are on you. You're on!

How can you help yourself at this most crucial point in your presentation? It's really quite simple. Use a visual aid. It gets your audience's focus of attention off of you right from the start!

What's the advantage of this? First off, it allows you to "adjust" to having the spotlight on you and eases you into your presentation. Your audience's attention is in fact re-directed away from you to a visual, enabling you to feel that much more comfortable during your opening moments.

## From Soup To Nuts!

Let me tell you a story of how I first discovered just how

effective this trick is. I was a rookie in the business world, working for T. J. Lipton Company (yes, the tea and soup folks), and was asked to make a presentation to a group of managers. The presentation was about a new system for writing job descriptions, and my task was to introduce the framework for this new system to the management team. Was I scared? I think "terrified" would be a more apt reflection of my feelings.

On the morning of my presentation I had a copy of the Agenda prepared for each of the participants. I placed it on the table in front of each person. One by one the managers arrived and took their seats. Soon they were all seated and the moment of truth had arrived.

The first trembling words out of my mouth were, "Good morning ladies and gentlemen. Would you please take a look at the Agenda in front of you and I'll go over it with you".

They all looked down. Relief swept over me. Their eyes were on the Agenda, not me!

Now, that first fitful start at presenting may not have been the smoothest way to start a presentation, but it did get me over that initial hurdle. And it proved to be a valuable lesson in how to give myself a bit of a break during those first critical moments.

That was my initiation into the value of using a visual aid to assist me in increasing my confidence. I've used this "Agenda" trick countless times since then, and I'm always grateful that I was able to stumble onto this technique so early in my career.

I've always marveled at how it is always so effective at easing me into a presentation and enabling me to adjust to my new position as the center of attention. You can also be assured that this is a foolproof method of getting you (and your presentation) off to a great start.

Naturally, you can vary this technique to suit your needs. For example, you can have the title of your presentation as your opening visual on the screen. Likewise, a visual with a question, statement or quotation that neatly fits in with the theme of your presentation would also be very effective.

Those are a few examples of how valuable visual aids can be in helping you to become a more confident and effective presenter. Let's take a look at a few more "tips" that you can add to your kitbag of ideas.

### What's Your Point?

Visuals will also enable you and your audience to "stay on track". You see, quite often your mind will tend to race ahead when you're presenting. Why? It's simple. You are quite naturally concerned with what you are going to say next. However, when you do this you run the common risk of "drawing a complete blank". And believe me this happens to many presenters.

If, however, you have your key points laid out on a visual aid you don't have to concern yourself at all about what point is coming up next. You'll have the key points right in front of you. You can simply use the points on the visual aid to trigger your mind into action. This also lets you add some additional thoughts around the points that are being viewed by your audience.

How does this impact your effectiveness with your audience? Will they see the four or five points that you're about to make before you actually discuss them? Yes, and that's just great. The points will keep each member of your audience right on track and automatically put their thoughts in the right "space" to think about the points that are "coming up".

Another approach you can use is to reveal one point at a time on a slide. This will keep your audience on track, and let you build your ideas without letting them read ahead. Remember, variety is the spice of life, so experiment with different approaches and visual effects.

## Hearing Is Believing

Additionally, your audience will not only hear your points they can also see them. This accomplishes one very important thing for each and every one of your audience members. It helps them to retain and recall your ideas. It has been proven that people who have seen, as well as heard a message, will remember it far better than if they've only heard it.

One of the most challenging presentations to make is one that is extremely complex or technical in nature. Quite often the facts are very detailed, and the message is unfortunately often lost. If you're faced with this type of presentation, visuals will help you immensely in conveying ideas that are complex in nature and help you to avoid a potentially catastrophic presentation.

To illustrate this point in the presentation techniques seminars I used to conduct, I often challenged people to describe a spiral staircase to the person sitting next to them. The "catch" is that they can only use words and no visual aids. Naturally, they wanted to use their hands to assist them in their attempts to describe a spiral staircase.

The outcome was very predictable. People struggled and strained trying to select some words that they could use to effectively convey their idea and create an image in their minds. However, once I told them that they could use a form of visual aid to assist them in conveying the idea, the task became far less formidable. Inevitably, each of them used their index finger to spiral up into the air, and in this manner they were able to quickly and easily get their idea across. It certainly drove home the point of just how valuable visual aids (and gestures) can be in assisting presenters and their audiences.

**A Noteworthy Note**

A form of visual aid that has helped speakers since days of yore is a set of "notes". Notes are something that can help you to smoothly present your ideas with all the confidence of a pro. Your written points will prompt you to unfold your message in a smooth, crystal clear and understandable manner.

Many people over the years have aspired to give presentations without the use of notes. They mistakenly believe that the pinnacle of a presenter's talents is best demonstrated when he/she delivers a presentation without using notes. I'd like to strongly refute that idea. Here's why. The real ideal to strive for is to deliver a presentation smoothly. One that gets your message across with poise and polish. This does not, however, preclude the use of notes to help you accomplish this.

Many of the outstanding presenters on television or other venues use notes. Nightly newscasters still use paper notes in front of them that are often visible to the viewing audience. They make no attempt to hide them, even though they are always reading their "lines" directly off a teleprompter. The notes are there for backup in case the technology fails them.

My message to you is simple. It's AOK to use of notes.

**You've Got Mail!**

Your notes should always be written in point form. This enables you to quickly glance down at a point. If you have a page full of text, you don't need too much imagination to realize the difficulties this can pose. If you fall into the trap of writing your notes out in full sentences, you'll often end up simply reading your notes. Why? Because you'll find it almost impossible to look down at your notes, find the next sentence you want to deliver, look up at your audience, deliver the sentence and then look down again for your next sentence without losing your place in your notes.

Have you ever been in an audience where the presenter read their speech from beginning to end? How did you feel about the presenter? You were probably not too impressed. Oh, the message may have been delivered smoothly, even if it was read. But, because it was read, it lost that human touch in the delivery that we all want to see in a presenter. We want the message to be delivered in a genuine, sincere and natural manner. And, reading a speech just doesn't cut it.

If someone reads a speech in front of me, I feel like jumping up and asking him to e-mail me a copy of their speech. I'd still get the message. I'd be able to read it at my leisure or just plain delete it!

There are however some presenters who are very skilled at using notes that are written out in full sentences. I have observed politicians using notes of this nature. Their notes are usually written in very large font and have only a few sentences per page. There is always an exception to the rule!!

**Practice Makes Perfect**

So, to help you to remember the points you want to get across and to help you deliver smoothly (without reading your entire speech), use notes that are written in point form.

And, to really feel comfortable and confident when using your notes don't forget to practice using them. One of my rules of thumb is that I practice using my notes four times before I actually use them in my presentation. In this way, I am very confident that they will work for me during the actual presentation.

Notes can help you to deliver your ideas, plus ensure that you don't forget some of your key points.

Win-Win

You can also use points on visual aids to act as your notes. This will:

- Free you up from having to use excessive notes i.e. put some of your points on a visual rather than in your notes
- Facilitate using gestures to refer to your points (naturally) that or on a screen (or flipchart/whiteboard)
- Provide a supportive "roadmap" for you to follow
- Make your ideas that much more interesting for you to present... and for your audience to receive

**Rules Of Thumb**

One of the factors that really boosted my confidence as a presenter was when I knew that I was doing something "right". When I was learning the art of presenting (and my delivery wasn't as polished as other presenters), my confidence grew in leaps and bounds because I knew I was incorporating into my presentations some proven design and delivery techniques that would help me to get my message across. This included, to a large extent, the design and use of visual aids.

If you incorporate a number of the following points into your presentations I guarantee that your confidence will soar on your very next presentation. You'll be that much stronger as a presenter because you'll be using some proven and effective techniques to get your message across. Techniques with attitude!

Here are some essential rules of thumb that you can use to help you design effective visuals:

- Ensure your visuals aren't too busy, i.e. they have no more than six or seven points per visual.
- Add illustrations or charts whenever possible and don't just use words or numbers.
- Add color...even something as simple as underlining a title in a contrasting color can help add some visual pizzazz.
- Use points only for key words or phrases.
- Check to see if your text is large enough when displayed on the screen.
- Use a picture/image with no words ... you can talk to this and there are many powerful pics available free on the web.
    - Diagrams should be broken into parts instead of showing an entire end-to-end diagram.

Remember, visual aids can be an invaluable asset to both you and your audience if you design them with an eye to clarity and variety.

However, each type of visual aid has its own set of effective attributes and features. The rest of this Chapter will take a closer look at some common visual aids and show you how to incorporate them effectively into your future presentations.

If you're aware of some of the strengths and weaknesses of

the different mediums, you'll feel that much more at ease when you do a presentation and incorporate visuals. In essence, you'll be comfortable with your visuals and be able to take full advantage of their strengths. Let's take a look at some of the pros and cons associated with the three most common visual aids i.e., whiteboards, flip charts and images PowerPoint slides.

## Whimsical Whiteboards

**Pros:**

- Good for "building ideas" and keeping the audience with you as you unfold your points.
- Seems spontaneous (even if it is planned!)
- Casual/informal– whiteboards have a relaxed and unpretentious look.
- Inexpensive. After the initial purchase it's just the cost of a whiteboard marker.

**Cons:**

- Can slow the pace dramatically while you are adding some points to the board.
- Sometimes a presenter turns into a "teacher" without thinking about it. Sometimes, your audience won't like this lecture style. Adults often don't like to be treated like "students".

Keep these points in mind:

- Be sure you have fresh whiteboard markers.
- Make sure your markers haven't run out of ink!
- Talk to your audience, not the board, or they'll get bored.
- Don't use a flip chart marker, it makes a mess when you try to erase it! If you can.
- Make sure that you don't erase your key points that are on a whiteboard before your audience has had a chance to copy or digest them.

**Flip charts**

**Pros:**

- Perfect for capturing ideas from your audience and then referring back to those ideas as you move forward in your presentation.
- Adds visual variety, your presentation isn't solely reliant on computer-projected images.
- They can be prepared "on the fly", or ahead of time.
- They're cheap.

**Cons:**

- Often appear to be sloppy, that's because they often are sloppy.
- Flip chart markers easily run out of ink (or are out of ink), and presenters fool themselves into believing that their audience can really read the unreadable.
- Large audiences can't read the small print.
- Presenters fool themselves into believing that their audience can really read their unreadable writing!

**Plus:**

- You can post them on the wall for reference.
- You can prepare some ahead of time.
- However, watch out for the big trap which is to block part of the audience's view by standing too close to one side of the flip chart.

## Slides

PowerPoint slide shows can add sizzle to your presentation! The most popular means of creating and projecting computer slide shows is by using a computer software package called PowerPoint from Microsoft.

Even if you use another package, people will usually refer to it as a PowerPoint presentation.

Slide shows (virtual or in-person) have some very important pros and cons. Here are a few.

**Pros:**

- They are very colorful.
- They are legible. If your handwriting is bad, it doesn't matter.
- They offer animation.
- You can use a plethora of free images off the web and import them into your slides.
- It is a quick medium for both developing and changing ideas.
- They look very professional.

**Cons:**

- The slides are often "too busy". Think about having no more than six key points on a slide.
- There is too much animation. Don't overdo it, it will distract from your content.

## Props

Yes, sometimes it's great to bring an "object" or article to a presentation. This can also add to a virtual presentation.

One of my favorite and most successful visual aids that I like to use is an object that relates to the topic at hand. If you can "work in" an article into your presentation, you'll be pleasantly surprised at the very positive response and impact that it will have on your audience.

What kind of objects can you use? Anything that links to your message or topic will be effective. Just ensure that everyone can see it. Hold it up high if you have a large number of people in a live audience. Also, make sure that it really is connected in a meaningful way to the ideas that you are trying to convey.

For example, if you're talking about farming, show a potato or show off a bag of potatoes! If you're discussing virtual healthcare show an oximeter.

Bill Gates even released mosquitos out of a jar into a live audience during his TED Talk on Mosquitos, Malaria and Education!

Get the idea? Articles can have a tremendous impact on your audience. Why? Because people don't often use them in presentations. And that makes you stand out from the crowd if you use one. It also makes the ideas around the object/article stick in people's minds.

**In Summary**

Visuals can often help you to get your message across more effectively and more quickly. Additionally, they can make your presentations dynamic, interesting, memorable, exciting, colorful with panache. Okay, I got carried away!

Remember, it doesn't matter how important you think your message is, if you fail to keep your audience interested, they'll never "get it."

Finally, I'd like to emphasize once again the importance of practicing using your notes and visual aids. Your confidence level will soar if you take the time to practice your presentation.

In the next chapter we'll take a look at some specific situations that cause presenters to have nightmares. And you'll discover some proven techniques that will allow you to successfully tackle and overcome these stressful situations like a pro.

# CHAPTER 6

# DON'T SWEAT THE DISTRACTING STUFF

"While we may not be able to control all that happens to us, we can control what happens inside us".
- Benjamin Franklin

# IN THIS CHAPTER...

- Managing Problem Audience Members
- Turning The Negative Into Positive
- Overcoming Resistance to Your Ideas
- Getting and Keeping Your Composure

## Positively Speaking

Giving a successful presentation can be one of the most rewarding and enriching experiences of your life. You'll be able to feel a sense of euphoria and accomplishment that's difficult to match.

Conversely, it can also be a very crushing experience. experience. It can challenge your self-image and your self-worth like no other experience.

But take heart. There is hope and light at the end of the presentation tunnel. If you tackle challenging situations with a positive attitude, combined with some insights learned from the experiences of others, you can overcome any adversity and have a truly rewarding experience.

In this Chapter I'd like to share with you some ideas that will assist you in managing some of the most troublesome situations that keep presenters awake at night. Situations that can become nightmares and that send shivers down the spines of even the most seasoned presenters!

What you are about to discover are some of the most effective techniques available that you can use ether to avoid or to successfully tackle some potentially catastrophic situations.

We'll look at some situations that are bound to crop up in presentations that you deliver, but most important, I'll give you an action plan that will turn any of these situations into a positive ones for both you and your audience.

### The Antagonist In Your Audience!

**Situation:**

Someone in your audience angrily confronts you, openly disagreeing with something that you've said, and says so in no uncertain terms, calling your presentation "garbage" or using some other equally negative terms.

**How To Handle It:**

Some people, in any audience, just love to confront the presenter. They sometimes express legitimate concerns about the ideas being presented or they could be just looking for a "fight", or they are just argumentative by nature. For example, they may have resisted authority all their lives, and now they want to challenge what you say just because they perceive you as being in a position of authority.

Even if you suspect that they're just looking for a verbal sparring match, it's important that you view and treat their expressed concerns as genuine. This is *crucial* if you hope to come out of this confrontation as a "winner".

**Be A Class Act**

I'd like you to look upon these infrequent challenges as opportunities. They give you a chance to show some poise and class, and show just how professional you are in managing difficult situations. They'll also test your ability to verbally spar. The audience will be watching with keen interest how you handle the situation, and they'll have that much more respect for you if you handle it well.

You can successfully handle any and all confrontational situations in the future if you keep a positive mental attitude towards the audience member that's confronting you. Try to remain objective and view these confrontations as a challenge to your talents as a presenter and do not take them personally.

When someone openly challenges you, the entire audience is looking at your response to the situation and it is your response that is important, so keep your emotions in check. Seize this opportunity to showcase your talents as a presenter and as an individual.

Here, then, are some ideas that will lead to a positive outcome for you, the challenger and your audience:

### Count To Ten

Really, count to ten! If you don't you may respond by giving them a verbal tongue-lashing. And you will find yourself very embarrassed if you overreact in this way and the aggressive person from the audience backs off right away from the situation. You will be placed in the very unenviable position of having to apologize to the person who initiated the attack.

Your initial reaction whenever someone confronts your ideas should be to recognize that it's very much okay for them to challenge these ideas. It's healthy. They are listening to you. They have a right to challenge what you are presenting. So, don't get ticked off. Tell yourself to remain calm and cool. Don't let your emotions cloud your intellect. You need to be able to think objectively about the ideas that have been put forth as a challenge and how you can best respond. Do not let yourself become emotionally embroiled in the situation.

Also, please recognize that the antagonist is often one of a group. Even if the person is a jerk, he is still THEIR JERK so be careful in how you handle this person.

To sum up, count to ten. This will give you a chance to collect your thoughts and structure an appropriate response. It will also add some drama to the moment, and the silence will add some poignancy to your well thought out response. Don't feel you need to rush.

## Opportunity Knocks

One tactic that I've seen many presenters use successfully is to treat any challenge to their ideas as a unique opportunity to react in a very positive manner when they're confronted. They'll say, for example...

*"I'm glad you brought that up." Or...*
*"I didn't realize you felt that way and I want to thank you first for being so honest and forthright. Or...*
*"Let me see if I understand you correctly. You feel that..."*

This kind of response on your part will be the exact opposite of what the audience member expects. They're often spoiling for a battle...and you're giving them a compliment on their openness! This tends to not only throw them off their game plan, but it also allows you to demonstrate how much control you still have of the entire situation and your emotions.

The bottom line is don't let anyone get you emotionally involved. Keep your cool. Show them how much poise you really can muster in a potentially confrontational situation.

## This Is The Way It Is

Often when you're presenting new ideas, people naturally resist them. It's human nature to resist change.

People will often resist new ideas by pointing to events in the past to discredit these new ideas and back up their claims that your ideas won't work.

They might say something like the following:

*"That's what you told us last time and it just plain didn't work out. I don't believe that your new plan and idea has a chance in hell of working either."*

Whatever you do, stick to the facts that relate to the topic at hand. Don't get drawn into an argument related to all the problems of the past, something that is definitely counter-productive!

Also, you may not be completely informed about all of the details related to some of the previous problems, and they may want to ambush you with facts that you weren't privy to. Consequently, you may put yourself in the rather unfortunate position of going down the road of trying to defend some events of the past that are not defensible.

Tell your audience that what's past is past, and with 20/20 hindsight, maybe some of the decisions would have been made differently. Inform them that you're here today to deal with the reality of today's topic and how to move forward. You might, for example, tell them the following:
*"I can appreciate what you're saying. However, we're not here to debate what's happened in the past. I can assure you that we've learned a lot from that situation and would now like to focus on the task at hand."*

In essence, you're trying to tactfully and diplomatically steer people back on track to what will hopefully be a more productive presentation. Which reminds me of the definition I once heard of a diplomat. It went something like this. "A diplomat is someone who has the ability to tell someone to go to hell in such an effective way that the person is actually looking forward to the trip."

## It's Just One Big Misunderstanding

It's not uncommon for people in your audience to completely misunderstand what you're saying. They sometimes mistakenly attach a different meaning to what you are saying. This can quite naturally lead to some resistance to the ideas you're introducing to your audience.

If you sense that this is the case, it's important that you add some additional examples or thoughts around the point that's being brought into question. Doing this will give you a much clearer indication of whether this was simply just a misunderstanding, or if in fact the audience member really does have an objection to your ideas.

For example, how many times have you heard a member of an audience admit that they have misinterpreted the presenter by saying:

*"Oh, I'm sorry, what I thought you were saying was..."*

To get this kind of understanding the presenter had brought up more facts so that the audience member could get a much more clarity of the presentation points in question.

I've found it especially beneficial to elaborate on ideas when they relate to changes in the workplace. For example, sometimes people don't quite understand why these changes are being introduced. I'll try to anticipate their objections and elaborate on my ideas by giving the rationale behind the change. In this way, I give the audience full credit for understanding why the change is necessary, recognizing full well that they may still not agree with it.

## Tell It Like It Is

You may run into situations where you don't have enough background information to realistically defend a decision. Or, as a presenter you may not quite understand why a decision was necessary, or you may even disagree with it. I sometimes ran into this when I was a manager.

In this type of situation your role as presenter is to "tell" people about the changes that are about to affect them. I sincerely believe that it is folly for you to attempt to defend decisions that you don't have enough background information to draw upon. It will be much safer, and will be much more effective, if you say something like the following:

*"I'm not here to defend the merits of the upcoming changes, but to let you know what will be happening in the near future. I understand your concerns. What I'd like to do is remain focused on the purpose of this presentation, which is to describe how these changes will impact your Department."*

By expressing your thoughts with sensitivity such as this, you indicate clearly that you are unwilling to get into a heated argument, an argument that will almost certainly end up in a very unproductive situation to say the least.

**We Won't Do It!**

I was confronted at a meeting once when I asked the audience members to complete a suggestion sheet related to their thoughts about their workplace. This is how one of the people in the audience responded.

*"Why should we fill out this crap again? We've given suggestions in the past and nothing ever happens."*

A very valid point in this case! However, my role was to attempt to solicit some of their valuable ideas. What I did was to explain to them that I was certain that all of the ideas that they put forth in the past were of value and had merit. However, there is always budget, time and resource constraints that have to be considered.

Here is the concrete example I used for them to relate to. I had them imagine that they had to manage refurnishing their living room. They had $4,000.00 to work with. They saw a beautiful coffee table that cost $2,000.00. Although this coffee table was outstanding and had superior workmanship that would last a lifetime, they had to weigh the purchase of that coffee table with the other items that needed to be purchased. What would they do?

This example seemed to put into perspective the idea that their suggestions were of value, but "management" couldn't always act on them right away, or at all. I still encouraged them to offer their ideas and keep the channels of communication open.

By offering them this example and a new way of looking at things, I was able to successfully manage the objection. I didn't back down from my role. And yes, they did fill in their suggestion sheets.

In certain situations it's unproductive to enter into a discussion around contentious issues. However, elaboration on your ideas is often effective and can help you avoid unnecessary confrontations.

**Sorry ... I'm really dumb!**

One tactic you can use which gives you time to get your composure (and think through an effective/appropriate response) when you're confronted by an audience member, is to ask that person a question. For example...

*"I'm not quite sure I understand what you're saying?"*

It may not be exactly the truth, but it will force the person to repeat and possibly attempt to rephrase their objection and give you, the presenter, time to prepare a rebuttal.

Or you can rephrase their statement yourself, and ask the

audience member if you've "grasped the essence" of the objection. You might surprise yourself to find just how often you really have misinterpreted the objection. By using this tactic to gather your thoughts, you might also avoid an inappropriate response, because you really didn't understand the objection in the first place.

Sometimes a person may simply and spontaneously respond emotionally to something that you've said. For example, they might say...

*"That idea stinks. It'll never work!"*

It's important that you don't react to those kinds of emotional outbursts by automatically lashing back at the person. The key here is to discover the basis for their objection. Therefore, an appropriate response on your part to this kind of outburst might sound something like this...

*"Why do you feel that way?"* or *"Why do you say that?"*

By asking a question, you are really forcing the person to pause and think in an adult-like manner. In order to respond logically to your question, as opposed to emotionally, the individual will have to identify some concrete reasons behind their feelings. These reasons will give you some insights and background information related to "where they are coming from" so that you can respond appropriately.

Posing questions can indeed be a tremendous ally that you can use to keep on top of some very demanding situations.

## Solicit Support

What should you do if a person attacks your ideas and you're quite certain that they're not voicing an opinion that is widely shared by other people in the audience?

Reach out to the audience and seek support for the ideas that you've expressed. Ask the audience if they agree with the statements or the arguments put forth. Getting that additional support from members of the audience can more often than not curtail the attack from the audience member. Even if only one or two audience members openly come to your assistance, the aggressive instigator is now unsure of just how much more support for their point of view is out there and will usually "soften" his or her attack quite quickly.

This is a great tactic to use when you sense this is the case. You might, for example, ask...

*"Does everyone out there share this point of view?"*

There will also be occasions when you'll receive unsolicited support from one or more members of your audience. When this occurs, let them speak their mind! Allow these individuals, who are expressing support, to use their influence on fellow audience members to make your points for you. Their input will carry a lot more weight and influence people's thoughts more than anything you could say at that juncture.

So, if you feel there's support out there for your ideas, seek it out. If it comes, take it!

**I'm Just Doing My Job**

Sometimes you will be asked to deliver a presentation in a setting and under circumstances where you should expect resistance. Under these circumstances you should expect aggressive statements or questions related to the ideas that you are expressing. For example, if you are presenting ideas that do any of the following:

- Affect people in a negative way.
- Threaten the status quo.
- Ask for funding for a project/business.

- Require decisions that affect a department's budget.
- Request purchase of a specific product or service.
- Propose something that affects the lifestyle or livelihood of individuals.

Your "mental set" when presenting these kinds of ideas should be to expect challenges. They're going to be inevitable. You should expect resistance. You should mentally prepare yourself ahead of time. Be prepared, not shocked, when you come face-to-face with an aggressive posture adopted by a member of your audience.

There are also situations when you should indeed get resistance to your ideas if your audience is doing their job. For example, let's say you're requesting funding for a certain project from a group of Vice Presidents in a business setting. It is, in fact, the job of these Vice Presidents to challenge your request for funds. It's incumbent upon them, to fulfill their role to make sure that you've done your homework and have a solid business case that justifies the allocation of funds.

In this kind of presentation it's their mandate to ask you tough questions to ensure that they can make a knowledge-based decision. They need to make an informed decision based on the ideas that you are presenting. To accomplish this, they're going to ask you some tough, no-nonsense questions and expect knowledgeable answers. Do not get ticked off at them for challenging you.

Enter these presentations with an open mind and make very sure that you have done your homework. Think ahead of time what kinds of questions they are likely to ask and have answers ready for them. If you do, and answer their questions in a very informed manner, you'll look like a rock star!!

**Promises, Promises!**

Many of the presentations that I have delivered in the past related to IT solutions. As you can imagine, I ran into my share of people who resisted what I'm telling them because they have been "burned" with previous promises related to computer systems.

I have to present some ideas related to a "new and improved" system to them. Right! They've seen these promises dissolve as project deadlines come and go and poorly designed systems cause them nothing but headaches.

In the past I would try to explain why there had been so many problems with the previous system. I would, unsuccessfully, try to explain why the system didn't work as well as why it should have worked. None of these attempts seemed to appease their anger and frustration.

Then, in desperation, I once said, "I understand. I guess if I was in your shoes I'd be really upset, skeptical, and disillusioned as well!" Eureka. This is exactly what they wanted to hear. They wanted someone who really did understand that they'd been hurt and that they were still hurting. Once we had established this "understanding", we could quickly move away from the past and, in a clearer light, tackle the future.

I've never forgotten this lesson. Now, whenever someone has a legitimate "beef" that they want to air in public, I listen intently and let them get it out of their system. They feel better for it and I feel I've managed it in a professional manner and we're able to then get on with the "business at hand."

**Summary**

People who attack your ideas pose some of the most challenging and nerve-racking situations that you'll ever face. Your attitude has to remain positive when this occurs. Keeping your composure, and using your best judgment, should remain foremost in your mind.

And always, always keep in mind that the audience members are attacking your ideas, not you personally. This allows you to keep your emotions in check and respond to questions and statements in a professional and composed manner.

**The Persistent Questioner**

**Situation:**

There is a person in your audience who monopolizes the floor when you open it up for questions. He or she constantly has a raised hand, and their incessant questions are starting to clearly irritate other audience members.

**How To Handle It:**

We all know people who fit this description. We've all seen them i.e. the one or two people in an audience who constantly pepper the speaker with never ending questions. The questioner just loves to hear himself/herself talk.

You, the presenter, don't need to be an aficionado of body language to realize that these questions are beginning to agitate others in the audience. When the persistent questioner's hand goes up for the umpteenth time, everyone in the audience begins to groan and shake their heads. How do you deal with this situation?

**Don't Rush To Judgment**

First and foremost, remember that the persistent questioner may very well be genuinely interested in your presentation and not just asking questions to "show off" or be disruptive. Take it as a compliment that you're such a dynamic speaker that this individual is really enthusiastic about your subject matter and wants to find out more.

Therefore, no matter how difficult it is, it's crucial that you maintain a positive attitude towards this individual and the situation. Make sure that any irritation you may have does not show.

Why? Simply put, this person may in fact not realize that they are dominating the "floor". In their mind, they really want to get some more information from you. Therefore, be very thoughtful and tactful when trying to direct the presentation or invitation for more questions away from this individual.

## Tactful Tactics

Here are some tactics that you can use to make sure this type of challenging situation is kept under control:

- Tap your watch, or point to the clock on the wall, and say "I'm feeling a bit of time pressure". Then, look away from the persistent questioner and ask everyone to hold their questions (unless it's a question related to clarification of a point) until the end of your speech.

- Tell them, for example, that you'd love to keep responding to questions, but you're concerned that you'll not be able to cover everyone's need to hear some important information if you fail to cover the remaining points on the Agenda.

- Attempt to make the persistent questioner realize that there are other members of your audience who may have questions.

- You might transition away from the questioner by saying "We've had some good questions from ________, I'm wondering if there are some other people in the audience who have any questions."

Respond to this person's latest question, and then, without missing a beat, immediately:

– Turn away and deny eye contact to the questioner
– Start to discuss the next point in your presentation

This tactic will enable you to very adroitly regain control and get your presentation back on track. Don't look at the person, or even take a breath at the end of your response to the question. This could give them the opening that their looking for to ask yet another question. By "moving on" to your next point, you have automatically made any question that they may want to ask related to your previous point irrelevant.

- Indicate to the questioner that you'd really like to be able to spend more time responding to questions, however, you hadn't really planned to spend quite this much time on this one area of discussion.

- Ask the questioner if he or she wouldn't mind reserving any further questions until "break time", or until after the presentation, when you'd be delighted to discuss them with him then.

**Summary**

Remember (at all times) that the questioner has a real and genuine interest in your topic. However, you do have an obligation to your entire audience to make sure that their needs are also met and that their interest doesn't wane.

Your entire audience will be looking for you to manage the persistent questioner with finesse. However, they will also be holding you accountable and expect you to keep your presentation flowing.

## The Know-it-all In Your Midst

**Situation:**

One or more members of your audience knows more than you do about your topic. Yes... they really do!

**How To Handle It:**

Imagine that someone sitting in your audience has a Ph.D. in the subject you are presenting. I have run into this situation a few times in my career and it can be very unsettling.

Far worse, however, are those in your audience who wish they had a Ph.D. but don't! These self-proclaimed experts sometimes like to use the presentation forum as an opportunity to publicly exhibit just how knowledgeable they are in your chosen topic. There will, in all likelihood, also be people in your audience who have insights into your subject matter based on first-hand experience.

Let's take a look at some techniques that will help you to feel much more comfortable and confident when faced with the "experts" in your audience.

- Set the stage for your presentation very carefully. Be sure to tell your audience what topics you will, and (most importantly), will not discuss.

This immediately puts in place some boundaries around your topic and shields you from getting into areas of discussion that could cause you problems with the "expert". In other words, you're telling the experts that the topic isn't wide open, but has some pre-defined parameters that you're going to stick to.

Here's an example of how this careful staging can save you a lot of grief. Suppose, for example, your presentation is on the topic of "The Impact Of Airplanes On The Travel Industry Going To Remote Regions of The Planet". Quite possibly you'll have some private pilots in your audience. Anticipating this, it would be prudent to tell your audience that you won't be discussing such things as the types of airplanes that are used, but you want to focus on how commercial airliners have opened up new vistas and opportunities for the traveling public.

By providing this framework for discussion, you're indicating to the experts, at the outset, that you are limiting the nature and scope of your topic.

Sometimes, in a business setting, the experts in your audience have been directed by their Department to attend your presentation. And, if they have colleagues in the audience who know that they are experts in the subject you are talking about, their forced participation could be a form of embarrassment.

For example, some of their colleagues might say, "What are you doing here? You know all about this, don't you?" They quite naturally don't understand why the "expert" is in the audience, and how it could be of value to them.

To address this rather challenging situation, I'd be very "up front" with the audience vis-à-vis the experts. I'll indicate that I understand that certain individuals have some background and expertise in this subject matter area, and I would welcome their input.

What does this do? It keeps their self-worth intact. It acknowledges their expertise publicly in front of their peers and colleagues. It indicates that I'm not threatened by their presence (even if I am)! And, on the same note, it really does take the threat away because I have openly invited them to share their expertise.

At certain points in the presentation, I will, if appropriate, turn to these individuals and solicit their thoughts. This can be very effective, and really can add significantly to the success of a presentation.

## Let's Have A Beer

At one point in my career I had the good fortune to give a presentation in Switzerland. And not because I'm a chocoholic!! During the introduction, I discovered that a lawyer was a member of the audience. We were going to present some potentially controversial ideas, that had legal implications. A potential catastrophe was in the making for me.

To avoid any chance of a devastating blow, I confronted the threat head on. After everyone in the audience had introduced themselves, I acknowledged the person as being a member of the legal profession and indicated that I was sure he would have some viewpoints on some of the legal aspects of the presentation.

Then, I indicated that we wouldn't have time to focus on these legal aspects during the presentation, but I would really relish the opportunity to discuss this at length over a coffee or a beer. It worked. He never asked a question and I didn't sweat it. By acknowledging his expertise and professional status and by opening the door to discuss this at his leisure, I also took the potential need he may have felt to challenge some of the legal aspects of the discussion. A win/win situation. He got his beer and Switzerland was wonderful to me!

## Stumped?

What can you do if you get a question from an expert that causes you real problems, a question that really stumps you? Here are a few ideas that should help get you out of that kind of situation:

For example, someone asks you for some more detailed information and you really can't give them an answer to the level that they want. You really don't know the answer. I'd suggest that you tell them the following:

– *"I'm sorry, but I haven't had an opportunity to look into that yet"*, or, *"I don't know the answer right now, but I'll write down your question and get back to you with the answer."*
– Offer an "educated guess", or a "ballpark figure" if you can. However, be sure to tell them that it is just an educated guess.
– Bring some detailed reference material along with you and have it available at your fingertips. You'll be surprised how often you'll be able to quickly reference something in a document that will provide someone with the exact details that they are seeking. You can even do this during a break.

If you get a question that you really believe is too detailed, indicate this fact to the questioner. Tell them that although it's a very interesting question, it's really beyond the intended scope of your presentation. If, for example, you are giving an "overview" presentation, be sure to keep it at an overview level. This is why stating the AIM of your presentation is so critical at the outset.

Another idea is to bring your own experts along. This can really save you from a lot of sleepless nights. If you have one or two people that are experts in the area you're presenting, have them sit in on your presentation, and ask them to field some of the more detailed questions. This will not only compliment your audience, (indicating to them just how important they are and how important it is to you that they get their questions answered) it will also make your task that much less stressful.

Finally, anticipate questions. Sit back after you've developed your presentation and think about what potential questions you can get from your audience. This can arm you with some very useful information that you can use to respond to the "experts" in the audience.

## Summary

Hopefully, some of these ideas will assist you in dealing with the experts you'll face over the years.

Keep in mind, though, that although it's crucial to "do your homework" you can't know everything. There will be moments when you just plain don't know the answer.

Also, when you're doing your prep work, keep the AIM of your presentation foremost in your mind. Don't get caught in the trap of trying to research everything about your topic. Take your knowledge level to a depth beyond the level you intend to present, **but not to a level that's far beyond the scope of your presentation. If you get caught in the cycle of asking yourself "what if they ask this" and then look for the answer you will never stop.**

Then relax and welcome the opportunity and challenge of having experts in your audience!

## Boring Material. Boring Material. Boring Material!

### Situation:

The subject matter for your presentation is very factual and/or technical, therefore potentially very boring. You think that death by a thousand cuts would be better than presenting this stuff.

### How To Handle It:

Wouldn't it be fabulous if the topics you were asked to present were always exciting, thrilling, captivating and exciting? The reality is that more often than not, you'll be faced with the challenge of presenting some of the most boring topics imaginable.

Well, guess what, there are many, many ways of breathing life into this deadly material. What follows is a potpourri of ideas that will be sure to add some spark to this snoring material, a spark that is needed to keep your audience (and you!) awake and interested. If you are bored with your topic, you can't really expect your audience to get excited about it either.

Whenever I'm developing a presentation, I review the material I'm going to present with a very critical eye. What I'm looking for is that portion of my presentation that is the most boring, then I add some life to it. And, believe it or not, that section more often than not becomes the most exciting part of my entire presentation.

Give some of the following ideas a try. You (and your audience) will be extremely pleased that you took the time to liven up your presentation.

## Work The Room

If it's possible, try to get the folks in your audience participating and engaged. How? It could involve the following:

- Question and answer sessions
- Discussion sessions
- Group work
- Individual tasks at their seats

Of course, you can't always get people actively involved in all your presentations. For example, it's difficult to organize a group task for an audience of five hundred people. However, it's possible to involve them mentally by asking them rhetorical questions that they will have to answer in their own minds.

An example of this kind of question would be "How many messages do you get in a single day?" Do you see how this kind of question will stimulate people to be mentally involved in your presentation. It prompts them to think and be engaged.

Another great technique, which always works to break down the imaginary barrier between you and your audience is to have a "show of hands". For example, you could ask them "How many of you answer more than 20 emails a day?" It's very natural way for you to overcome boredom and involve your audience in a very non-threatening way.

## Add Some Sizzle To The Steak With Sizzling Visuals

Try adding some pizzazz to your presentation via creative

visual aids. Think about using one or more of the following to add some visual variety and excitement to your presentation.

- Graphics
- Photos off the Web
- Animation
- Equipment displays
- Pamphlets
- Posters on the wall
- Handouts
- Objects/articles to display or pass around
- Video segments
- Demonstrations

**Get Real!**

Try using real world **examples** to spice up your dry material. All too often we get caught in the bear trap of speaking in generalities. We discuss facts or ideas without giving an actual example of what it is we're talking about.

For example, if you were discussing how to complete a tax form that has changed since last year (could this get any more boring?) select a person who is in your audience and use his or her name in your example. "Ok, let's say that George here made a million bucks last year. How would that be reflected in the new tax form?" This adds some humor also.

At other times, tell a story that relates to a portion of your presentation that is very dry. For example, if you were discussing the pros and cons of managing your time, you might weave in a disastrous story of someone who didn't plan his or her day.

Use a "real" name to add life to the story. For example: "The day started out like any other day. Joe walked into his office and started to check his e-mail. He began to reply to an urgent message when he suddenly remembered that he was late for a business meeting with a client. At that very instant, his telephone rang. Guess who?"

Get the idea? Make your presentations come alive by using an imaginary situation.

**It Was A Disaster When...**

Everyone loves a "war story". These types of stories can be extremely effective if you sprinkle them throughout your presentation. People enjoy hearing about disasters that have happened. It's related to that "let's hear about someone else's problems" thing! If you have some scars up and down your back that relate to experiences connected with your presentation topic, be sure to think of them ahead of time and build them into the presentation.

Alternatively, there are often some very humorous situations that you may have found yourself in that can add some laughter to your presentation. Just be sure that the story that you present has a direct connection with your topic. Don't just "throw in" a funny story out of the blue, it will backfire on you.

Here's a "potpourri" of ideas that you can put in your kitbag:

**Quotable Quotes:**

Go on the web where you can find thousands of quotes that will relate to your topic.

These witty and wise comments from famous people can really add some life and often humor to your presentation. People just love them and will often copy them down for their own future reference.

**Tips and Traps:**

Offering some quick tips and key points will always be well received. They are quick sound bites that will be a hit with any audience. Be sure to highlight them in your presentation by putting them in a separate section such as the following: "John's Top Ten Tips and Traps."

Your audience will really pay attention to these juicy little tidbits of information that you can pass their way. They are succinct, to the point and memorable sound bites.

**Personalize Your Points:**

– It is extremely difficult for your audience to maintain their interest and relate to your points if they don't clearly see how your content relates to them. To counteract this, you can drive home your points by personalizing your material as much as possible to the people in your audience.

For example, use the names of people in your audience whenever you can. I mentioned this earlier, but a caveat is necessary. When you use someone's name, it has to be done in a natural way, and not be overused. If your audience senses that you are doing it for effect or to curry their favor, they will not be pleased. However, if you use their names as you might in an ordinary conversation, it can be and extremely effective technique.

In the same vein, you can sometimes mention the name of an organization, company or department represented in your audience. This sends a strong message that you're aiming your presentation ideas directly at them and their business. Also try to include some examples that connect your ideas to the roles that people have in their organization. Tell them how they can use your ideas in a very personal way to help them reach a goals.

**Summary**

Try to be as creative and innovative as possible when you're faced with the task of presenting boring, dry material. It isn't easy, but you'll get a lot of personal satisfaction and be personally rewarded by adding pizzazz into your presentations. Remember: Let your style drive your subject matter, don't let your subject matter drive your style!

**Dealing With The Non-Responsive Audience.**

**Situation:**

You're audience doesn't respond when you ask them if they have any questions. They are very docile, and don't show the slightest interest in what you're presenting.

**How To Handle It:**

Quite often you'll face an audience that seems to be "reserved" about expressing themselves. They don't ask questions. They are non-responsive when you ask them point blank if they understand what you're talking about. In fact, you wonder if they are indeed dead from the neck up!

It's important to recognize that no two audiences are alike. You may, for instance, give the same speech to two different audiences and get two totally different responses.

The first audience is very open and responsive. They ask lots of questions and seem to be getting value from your ideas. The second audience, even though the same presentation material is presented to them, may respond totally different. They're unresponsive, disinterested and quiet. What to do?

We have to look at three dimensions in a situation such as this, they are...

- The presenter (you)
- The audience (them)
- The topic/content (it)

Let's examine some very special ideas that relate to each of these dimensions, ideas that will help you to create a successful outcome.

**Get Pumped**

Are you psyched up for the presentation? Remember, you're the key player in the success of the overall presentation. It's important to make sure that your interest hasn't waned. Here's a checklist to go over.

Are you:

- Not really interested in the topic?
- Drained because you've presented this speech so many times that you're personally bored stiff?
- Pre-occupied with personal problems? For example, your car is in the shop and you're awaiting the call to find out how much it will cost to fix that lemon!
- Sensing that your audience isn't interested, even before you start?

Let's face it, if you seem disinterested in the topic or the audience, and your audience senses this, they will respond in kind.

To combat this tendency, try to think of as many reasons as possible to get excited about presenting this topic. Try to psyche yourself up into a positive mood. You may need to give yourself a mental "pep talk". In situations like this, I tell myself that this will be the best presentation I've ever given in my life.

And I really believe it!

If you view this as a personal challenge (to get yourself in a positive frame of mind), you'll be very surprised at just how much your own attitude and excitement will be transferred to your audience. Try it and you will have some quite remarkable and memorable results.

## The Audience Is Terrible

Occasionally, the people in your audience, on a given day when the moon and stars are in a certain alignment, are not as enthusiastic as you might have expected. Quite frankly, you could be doing cartwheels and spitting nickels in front of this audience and they would simply yawn and look at their watches.

What do you do? Tell them they're terrible and leave? No! Don't ever give up. Keep your enthusiasm high. Do not overreact to their apparent apathy. In fact, you might be pleasantly surprised at the real enthusiasm that lurks just below the surface of this kind of dud audience.

For example, after giving a speech, quite often I've been approached by some of the people in the audience who had seemed to be the least interested in what I had to say. However, they've surprised me and told me just how enthusiastic they were about the ideas presented. Show some emotion and enthusiasm when you're speaking for goodness sakes! Even thought some people in the audience may have trouble showing theirs.

## Your Topic Shouts...Boring!

Sometimes, the material you're presenting can cause you

major grief. Your audience will quite often be extremely bored if they can't make a connection with what you are saying. Plus, if the level of the material you're presenting doesn't meet their expectations, you can find yourself directly in line with the proverbial stuff that hits the fan.

For example, you'd better make sure that your speech or presentation is correctly titled. If not, it could be misinterpreted, leading people to believe that they will be hearing some ideas from you that you are not, in fact, presenting.

Ensure that the message and ideas that you are presenting are relevant to the needs of your audience. Describe situations that they would encounter.

The three dimensions just described (presenter, audience, topic) can combine to lead to the ultimate success (or the dismal failure) of a presentation. It's crucial that you work on all three dimensions in your presentation to meet the challenge of a potentially unresponsive audience.

## Meeting The Challenge of No Questions

First, give the people in your audience time to formulate a question. Giving them at least 10 seconds may seem like a painful amount of time for you, but it really isn't a long time at all. Count to 10.

Sometimes, you will find that your audience just won't have any questions. You've done such a fantastic job of explaining everything, that they completely understand what you've told them and they don't have any questions at all. How many times have you been in an audience and really haven't had any questions for the presenter? Everything was perfectly clear, and you really didn't have a question. So, give it up, let it go and move on! Simply say... *"Fantastic! Let's move on."*

There are other times, however, when you're sure that there are some folks out there who have a question or opinion on what you've said. People are sometimes simply reluctant to speak out and ask questions in front of a large audience, or in front of their boss or peers. To overcome this reluctance you can turn to an audience member, who you believe has a question, and ask them if they have one. Or, try the following:

- Ask your audience if they have any thoughts or concerns about what it was you've presented, as opposed to asking specific questions.
- Pose a hypothetical situation related to your topic and then ask them how they would handle it (this is best thought out ahead of time as a backup).
- Give them some "for instance" questions related to the ideas you've discussed. For example you might ask: *"Do any of you have any questions on how best to handle people waiting in a line who are really annoyed that you are taking so long to serve other clients?"*
- Ask them if any of the points in your presentation were confusing, or if there are any points that they would like you to elaborate on.
- Ask them to write out a question or two on a piece of paper and tell them you'll address their questions in a few minutes. This is a super technique if you feel people will not respond to an open call for questions!
- Under extreme circumstances, have a "plant" in your audience i.e. a friend or colleague who you have collaborated with ahead of time to ask you a question.

Usually this is all you need to prime the pump, i.e. the first question gets things rolling. And, you can look particularly brilliant when you answer it with such poise and confidence.

Personally, I don't feel comfortable with this technique. But it can work in some situations where you anticipate an audience that will be extremely reluctant to ask you questions.

Remember...

The mood you create when you open up the floor for questions really sets the stage. For example:

Tell your audience how important it is that they ask questions.
Tell them that you have set aside some significant time for them to ask questions.
Tell them it is the one way that you can be sure that their needs are being met and they understand the presentation content.
Tell them that you've been talking far too long, and now it's their turn.

Then, when that very first important question finally comes your way, tell the questioner "that's a great question"! This will set the mood for all the other questions.

## Summary

Presenting to an unresponsive audience is one of the most unsettling and challenging situations you will face as a presenter. You will never be quite sure how you are coming across, not sure what they're thinking. Naturally, you will tend to think the worst of yourself, that you are the most boring/lame/incompetent presenter they've ever listened to.

Do not think the worst. It will only warp your view of your audience. Try some of the techniques described in this section. And, above all else, have a plan ahead of time that you can implement if your audience is in fact unresponsive.

## A Mixed Bag

### Situation:

Every audience that you face is made up of unique individuals. And each of these people will have varying degrees of knowledge, expertise and life experiences in the subject area that you are presenting. Therefore, there will be various levels of understanding and appreciation of the topic at hand, plus different expectations vis-à-vis the level at which you will talk to them. How can you successfully manage this situation?

### How To Handle It:

Whenever you design and develop a speech you do so with a certain set of assumptions in mind. You have no choice.

You have to assume a certain level of understanding. You also have to assume that your audience will have a certain amount of knowledge related the content that you are presenting.

For example, if you were speaking to a group of people at the Ph.D. level, you would adjust your content to assume a certain level of understanding. If you tried talking to the local junior baseball team using the same words they would probably throw something at you.

The assumptions that we all have to make can, however, lead to problems. You may be using certain colloquialisms that they are not familiar with. Or there may be specific information that you assumed they would relate to, that you're using as a basis or reference point, and they're not at all acquainted with it.

In essence, you're often facing an audience that is not at all homogeneous. There is a mix of people. People, for example, with different needs from different departments within a company. People with different knowledge levels. People with varied levels of interest in your topic. And, of course, people who have different experiences and expertise related to the subject matter.

What are you to do with all these variables and different dimensions in one audience? Here are some top tips that will guarantee you have a good shot at connecting with any audience you face, and at the same time meet their expectations.

**Set The Expectations For Your Target Audience**

The AIM of your presentation is extremely important when you know that there will be a large cross-section of people with an equally varied amount of expertise. Make your AIM as specific as possible. Take time to articulate it, and frames it, in a way that communicates very clearly what it is you will be discussing.

Of equal importance in situations like this is the OUTLINE or agenda of your presentation. It should spell out exactly what areas you'll be discussing and what level of detail you'll be delving into. Make sure that the scope and purpose of your presentation is very clearly defined at the outset.

Also, acknowledge in front of your entire audience that you recognize that there are various interests represented and various levels of expertise or experience. You want to do your best to accommodate all their needs. This sensitizes them to the fact that you want to take care of the needs of all members of the audience. It also helps them to control questions that they may be too detailed or esoteric. However, there is always one person who simply wants to impress people with how smart they are by asking a question that only someone with a doctorate would understand!

Reinforce the purpose of your presentation. Tell them the level of depth that you intend to take it to. And just as important, tell them the level of depth that you won't be able to discuss during the presentation. This is key if you feel this could pose a serious time limitation problem or could open it up into areas that you have little expertise in.

Many presentations are designed to provide people with a high-level overview of a topic. If the questions are getting "too deep", or aren't as relevant to everyone in your audience, express your concerns. For example, encourage people to ask questions if they don't understand something, but ask them to remember that the purpose of the presentation is to provide them with an overview.

Or tell them that if they don't grasp everything it's AOK. Let them know that you're willing to spend some time with them after the presentation to explain the gaps or during a break.

**Lack Of Understanding**

**Situation:**

You've tried and tried, but some folks still don't get it. Some are still not grasping the fundamental ideas you are trying so desperately to convey to them.

How do you know that they are "confused"? It is usually reflected in their questions. That is a sure-fire way to judge the level of understanding that they have of the topic. What should you do?

**How To Handle It:**

First, make a realistic judgment call. You must make a clear call to move on at some point. If you don't, you will find yourself accommodating one or two individuals at the expense of the rest of your audience. You can't risk jeopardizing the success of your entire presentation by trying to be a "nice guy". But use some tact.

Be certain that your attitude is positive when dealing with this type of situation. Your audience will inevitably and intuitively, rally around one of their own if they feel that you, the presenter, is abusing a member of their "group".

So, the manner in which you move forward is a key factor in handling this pressing situation. Remember, you don't want to embarrass people. Here's an example of how you might address the situation where the level of detail is too deep for some people.

Make a blanket statement so that no one individual is singled out. For example: "It seems that the level at which I'm presenting my ideas is a bit more detailed than some of you were expecting. And that is certainly something that is no fault of yours. However, I do have to ensure that the level of my presentation meets, as much as possible, most people's needs, and so I'd like to move on at this time. I would however, like to spend time with anyone after the presentation who would like some clarification on any points that are unclear. But I'd ask each of you to please try to grasp as many of the ideas as you can as we go along, recognizing that some of you may need elaboration after this session."

This same technique can be effective as well for the bothersome person in your audience who tries to "show off" by asking questions at a level too deep for others to grasp.

**Summary**

Before you design and develop your presentation put yourself in your audience's shoes. Consider very carefully their expectations. What would you want to hear and see if you were sitting in their seat? At what level?

Then, design your presentation with your answers to these questions in mind. And, when you have an audience with varied backgrounds and motivations, you'll be well equipped to meet their needs.

## New Terms...New Problems

### Situation:

Your subject matter includes terms that you're sure some of the people in your audience are not familiar with. Or your presentation will be introducing new terms to just about everyone in your audience.

### How To Handle It:

Each business or industry has their own set of terms or jargon that are used to describe various aspects of their business.

For example, there may be some official forms that are referred to simply by their form number. Or there could be some acronyms used to abbreviate certain aspects of a business or product etc. For example, TSA refers to Transportation Security Agency and IBM refers to International Business Machines. Some are more universal, for example LoL! Often an industry has words that describe roles e.g. the movie business has what is called a "key grip".

All of these, at times, tend to be puzzling for those who are unfamiliar with the lingo. At times, you may also find yourself facing the challenging task of giving a presentation that is intended to "educate" people using terminology with which they are unfamiliar. One example would be an employee orientation presentation.

Managing these kinds of situations is relatively easy as long as you know the secret! Read on.

**Set Yourself Up For Success...Not Failure**

Here are some key ideas that will keep you out of hot water.

- Ask your audience to be sure to let you know, as you proceed with your presentation, if they have forgotten the meaning of a term or acronym. This gives them "permission" to ask in front of others without feeling embarrassed.
- Have a list of new terms, with their meanings, posted at the front of the meeting room on flip-chart paper. Or, you could have a typed glossary of terms that you can hand out to each person. In this way, they can reference terms or acronyms as you use throughout your presentation.
- Do not simply give the definition of a term or give the root words of an acronym only once and expect everyone to remember it. This can be extremely irritating when people can't remember, and you continue to ramble on using the term over and over again. So, have some material they can reference as mentioned, or make sure at the very least that you reinforce the definition or meaning a few times during the course of your presentation.
- Ensure that the words you use to define a term aren't more technical or confusing than the word itself! Many times a dictionary definition simply adds to the confusion. Don't hesitate to use your own words to put the definition in layman's terms that any person can understand.
- You can often make a word easier to grasp and remember if you mention the root word or associated words from which it

is derived. For example, the root word for lectern is lecture.

## Summary

Some members of your audience will be very sensitive to the use of new terms that they are unfamiliar with. They often won't say anything overtly during your presentation. However, they will have lots to say to others after your presentation about "all the terms she/he used" that they couldn't understand.

## Drawing A Blank

### Situation:

You're in the beginning, middle or end of your speech and suddenly your mind goes blank, it turns to mush. You have no more thoughts in your shriveling brain and are as close to brain dead as you can imagine. You are about to have an out of body experience. This might even be a good thing at this moment! If this were to happen to you at work, it could very well be called an out-of-job experience (:

### How To Handle It:

If this has happened to you join the club! It happens to most speakers at some point in their public speaking journey. The good news is that it's not unusual or out of the ordinary. You're not alone in experiencing this unsettling phenomenon. The bad news is you never know when it will strike. The reasons why presenters draw a blank are not really known. I believe that it is related to the fact that our mind is being stimulated in so many ways when we are speaking in front of a group that it sometimes gets distracted and forgets to get to the next "package" of material to be delivered.

It's really not all that hard to imagine this happening occasionally when you think of all the things that your brain has to process as you are doing your presentation. When you think about it, it's easy to get distracted during a presentation. All kinds of thoughts can run through your mind. For example:

- Why is that audience member falling asleep. Am I boring?
- Why do they all look so confused? Is it me, or did the words "good morning" bewilder them?

What is next in my presentation... I haven't a clue!
Why are those people dropping off this call?
Should I respond to the comments now or later?

Is it any wonder, with this litany of thoughts that we try to process, that we sometimes forget what we want to say next. The bottom line is that this will happen to you, my friend. However, let's take a look at what you can do to make sure that you recover as smoothly as possible.

**Pass The Buck**

Ask your audience if they have any questions. This is a fabulous "stall" tactic that I can personally vouch for. Why? Because it gives you time to get your composure and gather your thoughts.

You see, the silence that follows after you've asked, *"Do you have any questions?"* seems quite normal to your audience. People need time to formulate a question. As far as they are concerned you have simply found a point in your presentation where you thought that they might have a question or two. Little do they know that you had really drawn a blank and are using this ruse to get you out of a jam!

What do you do if you feel that it is just plain inappropriate to ask if there are any questions when you have drawn a blank? Here's another trick that will let you quite naturally stall for time without the audience knowing it.

Say to your audience *"There was one other thing that I wanted to mention."* Then, touch a finger to your forehead as if trying to "rattle your brain" into thinking of something that you forgot. Seize this moment to gather your thoughts about what it is you really want to say. Get your thoughts back on track and simply add, *"No, its escaped me."*. We do this all the time in normal conversation, so nothing dubious seems to be happening.

What you have done is given your audience the impression that you are thinking about something else you wanted to mention, while all the while you are gaining your composure and getting rid of the blank in your brain. In effect this ploy gives you "permission" to pause and gather your thoughts without feeling any pressure at all.

## The Train Has Left The Station

Sometimes our feeble mind really is blank. In fact, it is so blank that you can't remember any of the deceitful tricks that you have just read about. Now what?

When you can't think of anything else at this point, tell them the truth. Yep, just like George Washington with the old cherry tree routine. You could say something like *"Sorry, I've just lost my train of thought for a second."*

Sure, it's a little unsettling and embarrassing for you. However, it's ten times better than saying nothing. Why? Because by telling your audience that you're trying to take a moment to collect your thoughts you have given yourself permission to do so in silence. If you don't say something, anything, your audience gets really uncomfortable.

They may even think that you've "lost it completely". And that, my friend, is not what you or they want at all. They have a need to know what you are thinking, so convey it and they will be completely understanding and empathetic. Each and every one of your audience members has had this same thing happen to them.

## Summary

As you can see, there are a number of very effective techniques that you can use to get you through this dreaded situation. Techniques that the pros use more often than you have probably ever realized. The key thing to keep in mind is that you have to tell the audience something. Effectively, you are also buying yourself some time to gather your thoughts and move ahead. And if you are quick enough, sneaky enough, they will never suspect for a moment that you really did have zip going on in your brain.

## Distracting Distractions

### Situation:

Someone or something distracts the attention of your audience away from what you are saying.

### How To Handle It:

Remember, keeping even one person's complete attention during the course of a normal conversation is usually a challenge. Keeping the complete attention of an entire audience at all times is something that is just not going to happen. Especially when they are checking their devices!

The best that you can hope for is to try to minimize the impact of these extraneous distractions. You will never eliminate them altogether. You can't control everything that goes on around you.

**Talk 'Til The Cows Come Home!**

Sometimes there are circumstances that happen that will result in the loss of your entire audience's attention. Here's an example:

I was giving a presentation at a retreat in the middle of farm country. Yes, the place was beautiful and serene. Not a cloud in the sky, a babbling brook nearby, the farmer out in his field and cows in the meadow. Picture postcard perfect!

Idyllic that is until the cows, being naturally curious animals, ambled over to see just what was going on. And, because the only windows in the presentation room were across the back of the room, I was the only person in that room who could see the cows in the meadow moseying over towards us. Soon, there were about forty head of beef cattle staring at me with their huge eyes and with their slimy noses pressed against the windows.

Since I was the only person in the room who could see these enormous creatures, I decided to continue my presentation in the hope that these massive bovines would get bored and move on. This seemed to be a logical plan until one of them moooooed...really, really loud!!

I then witnessed twenty plus people jump out of their collective seats so fast and high that it looked like their ejection seats had activated in a jet fighter! Needless to say, my audience did lose their concentration! How did I handle it? We called an impromptu coffee break. I also called on someine to ask the farmer to herd the cows to another part of the pasture (:

**Kung Fu Fighting**

Another distracting moment that happened at my expense was when I was doing a presentation in a hotel ballroom. The huge ballroom was divided in half by a supposedly soundproof, expandable folding wall. I had about 150 people in my audience, so we were using only one-half of the room. Another group was on the other side of the wall. The problem was the other group.

The other group was a karate club consisting of about seventy-five, out-of-control members. About halfway through my presentation these folks decided to attack the dividing wall and do some practice kicks against it. Oh, and by the way, there is one thing that Kung Fu aficionados do when they kick at something, they let out a guttural, blood-curdling scream.

Surprise, surprise. What do you think my audience did when they heard the combined roar of seventy-five people screaming at the top of their lungs in the next room, immediately followed by the slamming of 150 feet into the room's dividing wall, which swayed inwards about five feet from the impact? My audience also let out a blood-curdling scream. Talk about a distraction.

How did I handle it? I went next door to ask them to keep it down...please (:

## It's A Dog/Kids/Doorbell Day

So what kind of distractions can you expect when presenting in a virtual call? No cows or karate club members next door. In fact, nothing that can lead to a major distraction. Wrong!

How about:

- Dogs and cats
- Kids
- The telephone rings
- The doorbell rings
- Someone yells to see what you're doing
- Your network goes down
- Etc. Etc.

These are just a few examples of some of the countless distracting situations that I have run into. Let's take a look at some others that might happen in a live situation and see how you might handle them.

## Side Conversations

Here's the situation. Two people in your audience are talking in whispered tones, sharing something on their iPhone, but they are obviously being heard by others in the group and are causing a distraction. What to do?

I'd suggest, first of all, that you don't panic and overreact and say something like: *"Hey, if you've got something to say why don't you share it with all of us?"* This probably isn't the most effective approach.

Chances are that their conversation won't last long, and they'll soon give you their full attention once again. Haven't you found yourself from time to time having a brief conversation with someone sitting next to you in a presentation and sharing a text message?

If you try to curtail this potentially brief conversation right away, you risk embarrassing the two individuals involved. In fact, they may have been discussing something related to your topic. It would be tragic if you "lost" their support because you reacted too quickly.

However, if it does persist, you need to take some action to prevent it from continuing at the expense of the rest of your audience. And here is a truly effective action that you can take that is almost guaranteed to work and is so subtle that it won't cause any potential embarrassment.

Simply look directly at the people who are engaged in the side conversation. That's right, stare right at them. Don't take your gaze off them even for a second. Every time they glance up at you, you are staring right at them. Believe me, they'll get the message in no time and curtail their conversation very quickly. It's simple and it works.

### Sleeping

Someone inevitably will fall asleep in a presentation you are conducting... whether it's virtual or not. Or you will see someone yawning with eyelids shutting and they are really struggling to stay awake.

First things first. Remember, you can't always interpret this behavior as a reflection of the lack of interest in your presentation (unless your entire audience is asleep)! They may have a newborn baby at home, or they might have flown in on a red-eye special from out of town. Who knows? If, however, a person does fall asleep, let them nap for a while. They probably need it. And most of all, don't take it personally.

On the other hand, if they are snoring or in a deep sleep, you can try:

- Snapping your fingers together to emphasize a point you are making.
- Slam your hand on the table in front of you to add drama to a point.
- Raise your voice.
- Initiate a conversation with the person sitting next to them.

As you are trying these tactics it's important to look right at the person sleeping. If the noise startles them from their slumber for even a split second, and they look in your direction, they'll see you staring right at them. This will be, to say the least, most unsettling. Chances are they will shake themselves awake and won't nod off again.

What do you do if these gentle tactics don't work? Let the person sleep. You're a presenter, not a disciplinarian. You don't have to hold yourself accountable for the individual actions of adults in your audience. They make their own decisions on their own conduct and behavior.

**Outside Disturbances**

Sometimes you will run into situations where people other than the members of your audience will be causing a disturbance and distracting your audience's attention. For example, I have experienced workers replacing florescent lights, electricians fixing thermostats, people installing room fixtures, roofers tiling a roof and waiters clashing dishes. The list is endless.

If you run into situations like these (and you will), don't panic. Try to ignore the disturbance if it seems like it is only going to be temporary or of a short duration. You might also make a witty remark to your audience about it if it persists for a while. The fact that you have acknowledged the disturbance in front of them will relieve their concern about the disturbance.

If, however, the disturbance persists you must take action that will prevent the situation from continuing or escalating. You might ask the people or the person who is causing the disturbance how much longer they'll be before they are finished their task. I'd suggest very strongly that you do not confront the worker directly if you determine that it is going to persist for some time. Why? Because they are "just doing their job". And, they'll sometimes tell you that in so many words.

I suggest that you find someone who can "chase down" the person who has requested the work that they are doing. For example, you might phone your contact in an office building, the banquet manager at a hotel, or the receptionist in a lobby. Don't take it upon yourself to source out who is in charge of the work that is taking place, use someone else to do this for you.

This allows you to quickly return to the presentation room and continue with your presentation. You might even be fortunate enough to have someone in your audience who will come to your aid and volunteer to find a person in authority. Or, you could ask one of the more responsible people in the room to step outside with your for a second and ask them in relative privacy to find someone for you who can remedy the situation.

Sometimes all of this will be to no avail. If you can't stop the disturbance, you'll have to do your best to work yourself and your audience through it. Or try to move to another location if that is a feasible option.

### Cell Phones

I suggest you don't ask people to turn them off. It sounds authoritarian and isn't the best mood setter at the start of your presentation. These days most people have their phones set to "vibrate" or have them turned off in a public setting. If not, the audience will react to any disturbance. End of story.

### Summary

Distractions will test your metal. Distractions are, well, distracting. Try to keep your cool. And remember, when it's all over you will have a great story to tell over a beer about the horrendous experience that you just went through. It's always easier to laugh about it afterwards, so put it in perspective.

Throughout this Chapter I've conveyed some options to you that you now have at your disposal related to managing difficult situations. Remember, above all, try to be diplomatic and tactful. It will only reflect positively on you. It doesn't mean that you'll be perceived as a spineless wimp, so check your ego at the door. It is a great opportunity to show some class.

# CHAPTER 7
# SELLING YOUR IDEAS

"You miss 100% of the shots you don't take." -*Wayne Gretzky*

# IN THIS CHAPTER...

- Identify crucial ideas that resonate with your audience
- Develop winning strategies for a sales presentation
- Uncover the needs of your target audience
- Create and environment of trust

We Are All In Sales

That was the message that was the mantra of a large international company I once worked for. And it wasn't a bad message once you understood what was being said. Of course, a lot of people in the company said... not me!!

Although many people think that selling is just for "sales people" we need to understand that at some point each and every one of us tries to sell our ideas to others. For example, if you are in a management or leadership position you will need to sell any number of ideas to other members of your team. Or, if you are a leader in some part of your organization you may be called on to share your expertise and convince others to follow your lead. Of course, if you are indeed in a sales team then the focus of your job is to sell and make money for the company.

This Chapter has ideas that will provide insights that can help you in whatever role you have. Some of the ideas are directly aimed at a selling situation with a prospect. However, if you are not in a direct sales role, I hope you can glean a number of ideas that will provide you with value when you are called upon to convince others to move forward with or adopt your ideas.

## Setting The Stage For Success

Preparation is a key to the success in any presentation and is absolutely crucial in any sales-oriented presentation that you undertake. Why? Since you are focused on <u>selling your ideas</u> rather than just <u>sharing your ideas</u> it is paramount that you understand how critical your content preparation is to "get to yes!" This Chapter takes a closer look at some important considerations.

I'll break this down into some critical ideas related to the Before, During, and After dimensions of your presentation.

# BEFORE YOUR PRESENTATION

## Get Background Information

One of the things I learned early in my career from a very savvy boss was that an Organization Chart (with the names of people in a company, their relationships and their roles) was an invaluable asset that we should get a copy of before any presentation in front of a new client or prospect. On the surface it didn't seem that important, but I very quickly realized how valuable it was and it's one of the very first things I try to get hold of to this day. I call it finding out "who's who in the zoo."

Organization charts can sometimes be obtained from the Web these days, but if not it is well worth asking a representative from the company for a copy. You can call or email the HR Dept. and explain you will be giving a presentation to some of their team members and they usually will email you a copy. It's often in the public domain.

Org charts not only show you the relationships of individuals, but also how the company is structured and organized to manage the business they are in. You will be surprised at how much insight you can garner from this. For example, you can Google the names of people who are going to be in your presentation to find out their background. You can also look them up on LinkedIn.

In one instance I discovered that someone I was going to present to had given a Ted Talk. I watched it, found out more about him, and was able to compliment him on this most remarkable accomplishment. Yes, it was flattering, but it was genuine.

**Requirements Gathering**

Try to find out as much as possible about the needs that the organization has ahead of time. You may be able to do this from a company representative that has asked you to conduct the presentation. You can even simply have an informal call with them or send them an email with a couple of questions related to the purpose of the presentation so that you can put your ideas in context.

You can also Google the company to find out as much as possible about their current financial situation (if it is a public company) or how they have positioned themselves in the marketplace.

Their website is an ideal place to start. Also, by simply Googling their organization's name you can often see the latest announcements related to their organization and get some great insights. By being current with their situation and reflecting this back to them in a presentation either formally or informally, you can demonstrate that you have done your homework.

It is also a great idea to Google the competition of the organization that you are presenting to. You may be able to see how they are positioning themselves in the marketplace against each other. Or you may be able to discover what challenges their entire industry is facing.

Why is this important? Because you need to weave into your presentation some content\material\ ideas that will RESONATE with your audience. What do they think is important for their organization? Who are their customers? Etc. The more background information you can gather the more confident you will be in creating the content for your presentation.

**You Are A Problem Solver**

Most presentations that are aimed at selling ideas/products/ services are problem solving in nature. Therefore, the more you can find out about the problem ahead of time the better prepared you will be in creating content that will resonate with your target audience.

For example, is this a problem that organizations of this nature have in common? For example, a lack of sales due to insufficient funding of brand marketing efforts? Getting beat out by the competition due to systems that are out of date? A need for more current and timely information? Etc.

What is the challenge or problem you will be addressing? If you have an opportunity, this is the key question you can ask of the person that may have requested that you present your ideas.

If you can't find out the exact problem, then you need to assume that you are presenting to solve a common problem or issue. You need to create your content based on what you have found to have been effective in previous presentations of this nature. You need to make a "best guess" as to what to present.

**Who Will Be In Your Audience?**

If you can get a sense of who will be in your audience that will be extremely useful in helping you position your message and the depth of your material you should include. For example, is it being delivered to a Senior Management Team or some junior managers? Is it to a mixed audience with differing experiences and knowledge levels on your topic?

If you are not sure, then create your content based on a level that will be understood by who you believe will typically be in an audience interested in your topic or offering.

I try to find out who will be in the audience from the individual who has requested the presentation or who is convening the meeting. I will also send them an email confirming my understanding of who will be in the audience and their anticipated interest in the topic. This will give this person an opportunity to clarify this if I have missed the mark.

One word of advice. Keep in mind that many of your prospects in an audience have already checked out your organization via the web, and they have often researched your topic.

Be prepared to discover that you have some very knowledgeable audience members these days. However, also be confident that through your presentation they will have an opportunity to get answers that they could never get from an online search.

## What Is The Purpose Of The Presentation?

Be sure to be able to clearly articulate the AIM or purpose of the presentation based on information you can determine in advance. What is the presentation's objective? What will a successful outcome look like? Are you trying to get "buy in" for a change that is happening, or is it part of a long sales cycle? Sales people sometimes ask "what is the call objective."

If you are presenting as part of a team it can be effective if a "team call" is set up before your presentation to confirm everyone's expectations for the presentation from within your group. This is done to:

- Discuss the AIM
- Discuss roles (presenters, note takers, question handling)
- Finalise the content of your presentation
- Ensure that you have as much background information as possible
- Solidify points where turnover takes place from presenter to
- Identify who will be in charge of fielding the questions

**Standing Out From The Crowd – Sell Value!**

One of the keys to success in many sales presentations is to be able to DIFFERENTIATE your company or organization from others. What sets you apart? What is it that you offer that is unique in the marketplace? How will you showcase this in your presentation?

Remember, if you are just like all the rest, you will only be competing on price. If you demonstrate "value" to your audience members' organization, then you can compete on a different level.

Think carefully about the value the prospect will get out of your product or solution. I believe in asking "value for value." How much value you bring to the table dictates how much it is worth to your prospect.

**Sell Benefits and Not Simply Features**

People buy benefits. Make sure that your content does not just contain a list of features of the product or service that you are offering. Benefits relate to the value I just mentioned.

For example, when you buy a car a sales brochure will give the miles per gallon. If this is an outstanding feature it should also provide you with the associated benefits. More miles per gallon means less wasted time refueling, and more money in your pocket. That's the benefit!!

Try to ask the "what is the benefit" question of what you are pitching and see if you can associate benefits to some of the main features.

# STORYTELLING

One of the most effective ways to make your sales-oriented presentation resonate with your audience is to tell a success story. Storytelling has proven to be an extremely effective way to make a presentation memorable, and also differentiate your organization from the rest. Why? Because no other person on planet earth has ever had the very same personal success story that you have. It is unique.

Look for areas in your presentation where you can begin a new segment with a story. You can for example simply relate a case study or success that another organization has had with your product or service. It is also an opportunity to add some fun memories into your presentation if something happened with your experience that was humorous in nature.

We often refer to these stories as "proof points" that relate to what you are selling. For example, how much money was saved by another company, how quickly were they able to implement your solution. Or what obstacles or challenges did they face and how did you help them to overcome these. These corporate experiences are often called case studies but that sounds so boring so make up a story around them!

What if you don't yet have a compelling story to tell. Use the words "Just imagine...." and then create a believable scenario where what you are selling can solve a problem. It engages your audience in a story that they can relate to. For example, here is something that you might say if you were trying to sell a Client Relationship Management solution. "Just imagine that you were trying to access information that would help you to improve your company's relationship with your key customers. You fire up your laptop on Monday morning and sit down to see what you need to do to make that happen. You discover that you really don't have the information at your fingertips to help you make an informed decision on how to move forward. This is a problem that many of our customers have faced and tackled head on with our offering. Let me tell you how we helped."

You get the idea. Build a story into your presentation and make your presentation memorable!

**Practice. Practice. Practice.**

Preparation is key to a successful outcome and nothing boosts your confidence as a presenter more than practicing what you will be presenting.

You will be surprised at how much it will help if you practice your presentation in front of someone else. Or you can record a practice presentation via your computer and review it yourself. Plus, you can also email it to someone who's advice you value and get their input.

Remember, be open to constructive criticism or even destructive criticism!! Check your ego at the door and listen to what others may have to say. It is meant to help. Sometimes people aren't as sensitive as they might be with their critiques so put it in perspective and don't take it personally.

Also, a word of caution. You are unique. Therefore, your style is unique. If someone is trying to change your style to the point that you will feel phony or uncomfortable don't do it. Thank them for any and all advice that they have freely offered, accept it in the spirit in which it is given, and then decide what to change or not to change based on your own best judgement.

One of the main reasons to practice is also to get your timing down pat. This holds true for any presentation, but even more so when you may be presenting to people from another organization. If you run out of time they will leave. Let me say that again... "if you run out of time they will leave."

They have no obligation to stay there and listen. In fact, they may have other business commitments that they need to attend to. You will not be able to have a smooth ending, and you will see people starting to leave and it will rattle your confidence. Don't set yourself up for this kind of failure. Practice your timing!

Also be aware that some people may have been "sent" to your presentation. They may not really want to be there so they will use any excuse (like your time is up) to pack up and leave.

**The Long and the Short Of It.**

There are many dimensions to presentations that are focused on selling and sharing ideas and helping a group reach a decision. However, there are essentially two types of presentations that you may be involved in related to traditional selling situations. Companies or organizations will usually be selling a service or a product. And these will fall into either a short sell cycle or a long sell cycle.

The short sell cycle scenario is where you are making a pitch that will in essence end in a yes or no decision at the end of your presentation or shortly after. This isn't just "do you want to buy one of the watches you see on my arm" presentations but a presentation that lasts up to an hour or two. The bottom line is that at the end of this kind of presentation you will be looking for a "buy decision" to be made based on this single presentation. You have one shot to make this work.

The other type of presentation is related to a longer sell cycle. This is a cycle where a major decision will take place and could take months of presentations and contract negotiations to finally conclude in a sale. These are usually ones where there are large amounts of budget money being allocated and it is often a very long and arduous process. For example, a prospect doing the due diligence necessary to making a buying decision related to purchasing a major computer system or even a corporate jet.

Each of these presentation types have their own challenges and opportunities. And each can be conducted in-person or via a virtual presentation. Let's see some ideas related to these situations.

**The Short Sell Cycle Presentation**

These are often "cookie cutter" presentations where you have a standard slide deck and present it many times to different audiences.

The one thing that differs between this and a long sell cycle is the time frame. With the short s sell cycle time frame you don't get a second chance. The sales pitch has to be done well, and there isn't really any opportunity to build a relationship over time with your audience. It can be tough.

However, this can also be very satisfying in that you don't waste time with prospects who can get you into a long process of decision making that can sometimes lead to frustration. You can clone your best ideas and optimize your calls to maximize your chances of success.

These types of presentations are often "pitch" oriented. They are short. Your message needs to be crisp. And you basically ask for an order or some action to be taken at the end of your presentation.

Caution! Make sure that you still personalize your pitch to your audience. Do your research and build in some new material every time by connecting with your audience. This will not only resonate better with your audience but will give you reason to be excited each and every time you present. Tailor your presentation!

A "call to action" is often part of the closing remarks of a short sell cycle presentation. You don't need to ask them to sign on the dotted line then and there, but you do want to let them know that you would like to find out if they would like to move forward with what you have proposed. You can give them a time line of what will take place if they say "yes" and what the next steps would be.

They will often want to "think about it" so don't pressure them and don't take this as a rejection. More often than not they will have a meeting after your presentation to make a group decision. Be sensitive to this and be sure to end on a positive note by expressing your appreciation for their time and consideration.

**The Long Sell Cycle Presentation**

These type of presentations often involve a team of presenters with various levels of expertise. We call these folks subject matter experts or SMEs.

One of the key considerations is that someone has to take the lead and organize and orchestrate the members of the team being called upon to present various segments. It is absolutely crucial to your success to let each person know what is expected of them. And, equally important, it is essential that they know how much time they have been allocated.

For example, I have been part of presentations where speakers before me went over their allocated time and chewed into my time allotment. I had to shed materials and slides from my deck on-the-fly! I was not a happy camper.

Please don't set yourself up for failure. Have a team meeting ahead of the presentation to make sure that everyone is on the same page as it relates to the content that they are expected to present, and the time allocated to their presentations. Tip: You can assign a time keeper to watch the clock and give a pre-determined signal when a speaker's time is almost up.

The other dimension related to this type of long sell cycle is that you often will be presenting your topic to different target audiences that are looking at your presentation through a different lens. They may be from different departments within the same company with different needs. Also, the level at which you're presenting often changes depending on the audience.

For example, I have presented a topic at a very high level to a Senior Executive Team in a Boardroom in the morning, and then have had to adjust the level of my presentation material to present to a team of Junior Managers in the afternoon. Followed by a more technical presentation to others the very next morning!

One other positive dimension to a long cycle sales initiative is that you will often have the opportunity to create a relationship with your prospects. This is often seen as the major difference between the long and short sell cycles.

# DURING YOUR PRESENTATION

There are many things to consider that will make your presentations a success during the actual delivery of your presentation. Many considerations of a general nature are covered in other parts of this book, so here I will focus on a couple of things that are often encountered in sales-oriented presentations.

**"Conversational Selling" Presentations**

I like to consider sales presentations as more of a conversation than a one-way presentation. Contrast this with a Ted Talk where the presenters are sharing life experiences with a passive audience. As a rule, they do not engage with an audience but tell a story or pass on some information of interest. The audience knows that their role is passive. The presenter knows that the audience expects their role to be passive.

Unlike a Ted Talk we have an opportunity to engage with our audiences (either virtually or in-person) to everyone's benefit. They can ask questions. You can engage in a dialogue. You can ask questions!

Tip: One thing that creates a conversational atmosphere is to start a conversation with one or two individuals before you start your formal presentation. It can be something as simple as talking about the weather. You can do this as others are joining the meeting and it can work for either a virtual or in-person situation. People see you in an informal and casual conversation and it puts them at ease.

Let's take a look at how to engage with an audience in more detail and see what you can do to optimize your chances of success.

**Questions and Answers**

I would recommend that you let your audience know that you will entertain questions as you proceed. You can establish this expectation early on when you review your Outline or Agenda.

Questions are your best friend. They enable you to get a pulse on what the audience is thinking, if they have any areas where they are confused, or if they need clarification of the points you are making. Say something like ... "Please feel free to ask questions as we go along."

The only caution is that someone may monopolize this opportunity at the expense of others. I cover how to handle this in detail in another area of this book but essentially make sure that you stay on time and on track so that everyone wins.

You can pose a question yourself now and then to create a dialogue and engagement. For example, at some point in your presentation you might ask your audience members "Is this something you run into here?" or "Are these the kind of challenges you have?" Etc. Think of these kind of questions ahead of time and build them into your notes.

Be sure to praise questioners from time to time with the phrase "That's a great question!" This can do a couple of things. It compliments the person and makes them feel good, and therefore encourages more questions. And it can also give you time to gather your thoughts for a second before you come up with an answer and respond! Make sure that you don't overdo this and say this in response to every question. It then starts to sound insincere and people will be turned off by it.

In virtual presentations there will sometimes be an opportunity for people to add comments or questions online as you proceed. It is usually best to have someone else manage these for you so that you can focus on your delivery. It is too challenging and distracting to try to manage these on the fly. At certain points in time your colleague can acknowledge the questioner and ask the question of you. This is a very acceptable practice in virtual presentation situations.

## Handling Objections

More than any other types of presentations the sales-oriented presentation will often result in people objecting to something that is being said.

There are many reasons for this including the fact that people resist change and what you are proposing will usually involve change of some kind. They may have been "burned" in the past and now are very sinical about embracing change once again based on false hope or expectations. As one person told me they have become "very jaded" when it comes to new ideas.

They may also express doubts about the validity of what you are claiming, or the anticipated benefits. Also, they may challenge you on how easy it is to implement, too costly, poor timing etc. etc.

No matter what the objection is, the manner in which you handle it that will leave a lasting impression with your audience. The key here is to show that you understand their concerns and offer possible ways to overcome the anticipated hurdles.

Sometimes the objection is difficult to handle because what they are saying is true. For example, your competition has a feature that you don't offer. I would suggest agreeing with this statement even though some pundits suggest to never agree or acknowledge the fact. If you simply ignore the audience member's point the rest of the audience will realize that you have ignored it and feel that you have been somewhat unresponsive to the person who brought up the point.

I think it is better to accept the point and then counter it with some of the other great benefits you have. Better still, if you know of a feature that you have that your competition doesn't have you can mention this and indicate that sometimes there are trade offs e.g. the performance may be degraded with their feature.

Here are some other insights related to handling objections:

- Don't "knock" or speak despairingly about their current system or product or solution. Members of your audience may have been part of the decision making team that approved something that now needs enhancing or didn't work out as expected. Don't put it down.
- Don't knock the competition. Why not? Because the competition may have recently announced some new features you are not aware of and you will show that you have not done your homework. Don't take a chance.
- Don't get dejected if your point gets rejected. You need to dust yourself off and keep going in a positive manner! Use it as a learning experience.

Do let others in the audience come to your aid if they are rebutting what someone is saying. Letting these "allies" have their say is a wonderful way to counter an objection without you having to say a word!!

Bottom line? Know the strengths and weaknesses of what you are proposing and be prepared to counter objections with some compelling facts.

# GENERATING A DIALOGUE

If you can get a conversation going about the needs related to your topic that will give you lots of information you can use to build a case for what you are proposing. In fact, some presentations are focused on needs identification.

Sometimes, and audience will be very willing to engage in a conversation. Sometimes it will be like pulling teeth. If you have trouble getting them to open up and engage with you try:

- Asking a specific person if they have any thoughts on the matter. I would suggest asking this of someone who seems open and chatty. I would not suggest directing this to any of the Senior Team members!
- Posing a hypothetical situation and ask how they might handle it.
- Have them think about how what you are proposing might fit into their environment.
- Tell them about something that you read related to their situation and ask them if that is something that they are experiencing in their company.
- Etc.

# DISTRACTIONS

In both in-person meetings and virtual presentations there are always opportunities for folks to become distracted while they are listening to you.

These include:

- Looking at texts from their spouse, their kids, colleagues etc.
- Answering texts from their spouse, their kids, colleagues etc.!!!
- Looking at other windows on their screen
- Typing something into their keyboard
- Laughing and chatting with each other with their audio turned off!
- Leaving their place in front of their computer so that they are no longer visible
- Etc.

Please be assured that all of these distractions will come your way at some time in your career. DO NOT let them rattle you. This is very normal. People will not be rivetted to your every word and sometimes need a break in a very personal way. They can multi-task!!!!!!!!!!
My advice. Simply keep moving on.

## Quit Drilling. You've Struck Oil!!!

This is what was written on a note that a colleague/friend of mine from our sales dept. slipped me during a presentation. I was three quarters of the way through my presentation when gave this to me.

In essence, he indicated that I had sold them on our idea and it was time to **stop selling** and start exploring how best to move forward.
How will you know if you should quit drilling? This will happen more often in a short sell cycle kind of presentation but it can also happen later on in a long sell cycle series of meetings.

Prospects will often give a "buy signal" that will be a great indicator that they have bought into your ideas. They will say for instance:

- That sounds great...
- I like the sounds of that...
- How would we go about implementing this...
- How soon could you start!
-

If you sense that this is the case it is probably best to quit drilling and don't continue with the rest of your planned presentation just because you have some slides left!

Start a dialogue about how to move forward and engage the prospect to get ideas **and ownership.** Letting a client offer some ideas and incorporating those ideas into your plans is a fantastic way to create a positive relationship that will help you overcome any obstacles that may arise.

Think of this the beginning of a wonderful partnership at this point, stop drilling and celebrate!

# AFTER THE PRESENTATION

Always, always send an email right away thanking the presentation participants for their time and consideration. This holds true for both short and long cycle presentations. You can also send a personal email to the individual who was the internal champion who sponsored you for the presentation.

Any follow up should also include any links to blogs or other supporting documentation that the participants can use to help them make an informed and knowledge-based decision. You can start your comments in this area with "As promised here are the links to additional information about XXX." This is a wonderful phrase you can use to further reinforce the trust that they can place in you to respond to their needs.

And, of course, offer to answer any more questions they may have that weren't covered in the presentation or that they would want more details around.

Your email is an opportunity to demonstrate some "class" so choose your words carefully.

What happens if you don't get the response and results you were looking for? It can be hard to keep going through all the *"No's"* on the road to a *"Yes."* However, some of the greatest thinkers, leaders and businesspeople of our time have encountered rejection. Think of the politicians who have not been elected or re-elected. Think of some of the space launches that ended up exploding on the launch pad! People learn from these experiences and persevere. Failure is what made them succeed.

And so, that is the end of this Chapter. I'll quit drilling (:

# CHAPTER 8
# CROSSING THE VIRTUAL DIVIDE

# IN THIS CHAPTER...

- How to set up equipment for success
- What location considerations are crucial
- How to use NOTES effectively
- Delivery tips and tricks

# VIRTUAL PRESENTATION INSIGHTS

## The "Zoom" Boom

Virtual presentations have become a platform for presenters ever since the COVID 19 pandemic hit the world. Prior to this, in-person presentations were the norm, although video-based presentations were given on an irregular basis.

These days you are more likely than not to find yourself presenting virtually in from of colleagues or clients. The remote working phenomenon is here to stay and so are virtual presentations. Adapting to life outside of the office includes virtual presentations.

Your virtual presentations will have some unique challenges. This lesson will take a look at some of those and what you can do that will lead to success.

However, please be aware that the success of any presentation you give still is dependent on the other considerations provided in this book. Presenting in a conference call is still simply sharing ideas. As I say... **your success in overcoming the fear of presenting is 10% presentation and 90% preparation!**

Here are some ideas on how to prepare for and deliver a stellar virtual presentation.

## BEFORE YOUR PRESENTATION

### The Equipment

The majority of presenters use the microphone and camera that are incorporated into their laptop or their desktop. For the most part, these are getting better and better and are more than adequate for most business and in-company presentations. They technology is becoming even more reliable so once you are all set to go just forget about it.

This is very much the attitude that pilots need to have when the fly in any airplane. After they have had a pre-flight inspection and tested some of the flight controls they assume that everything will go well in terms of the aircraft performing as expected. On very rare occasions there will be a mishap, but they are confident that they can handle it. You can be too.
There is a plethora of professional video cameras and mics in the marketplace.

For example, there are headphones with a mike and earphone combination from anywhere from twenty bucks to a couple of hundred. And, most of the popular camera manufacturers provide a huge selection of video cameras. These cameras can provide exceptional quality with features such as zoom lenses, wide angle lenses, high resolution HD and also high-quality sound recording.

This kind of professional equipment is often purchased when a professional recording is being made e.g. to promote an organization or brand etc. For example, a friend of mine is a professional videographer and uses professional cameras and lighting equipment to record public figures doing information sharing spots for public consumption. I am not going to dwell on adding professional-level equipment into your kit bag. I only suggest that if you want to look into what is available you can find something in your price range on the web.

What I would like to explore are some of the unique aspects of virtual presentations that should go into your preparation kit bag.

**The Invitations**

One thing to consider is the location of the people that will be on your call. With remote working these days they can be anywhere in the Country or around the world i.e. spanning several time zones.
Consideration needs to be made so that the time of your presentation accommodates the majority of the people at a time convenient for them. For example, be aware of when audience members in various locations might take breaks or eat meals.

And, hmmmm, be very sensitive to where the key players are located.

Calls these days can be made using any number of mainstream platforms including Zoom, Google Hangouts, and Microsoft Teams, Skype etc. You can simply start off using a free program and you can scale up depending on your needs. Be sure that your target audience has access to these popular platforms and choose one accordingly.

# THE EQUIPMENT CHECK

As mentioned, most of the equipment these days is very reliable. However, you should ALWAYS check it out in advance of your presentation.

Turn on your video and do a sound check. It only takes a few minutes and will give you confidence that you are all set from an equipment check perspective. I think we have all seen situations where someone's equipment was not working as expected during a conference call. Make sure it isn't you!

Plus, make sure your laptop is charged up or better yet plugged in. You really don't need the stress of having to scramble to find a plug when you get a warning that your battery is running low part way through your presentation. Plus, shut down any other programs or computers so that you get the best possible connection.

# THE VIRTUAL LOCATION

Let's look at some key considerations related to where you are going to set up for your presentation. Although these days people are very used to all kinds of backgrounds in a presenter's space including bookshelves, fireplaces, furniture, dogs and cats and kids etc. etc.

I did see a presentation with Oprah where she had her dog laying on the floor in the background of her presentation. Plus, another youtuber has his dog almost always in his videos. So, I guess just about anything goes.

Don't get me wrong. I do not advocate pets or kids in a shot. However, I also believe that people can multi-task and listen to what you are presenting while still checking out the titles of books that may be in your bookshelf. C'mon. We all do it!!

There are also apps out there that provide virtual background that you can use. Be careful though because they may consume additional bandwidth that can cause more problems than they are worth.

Position the camera so that you will be seen from at least the chest up instead of just becoming a "talking head." This will enable you to gesture naturally and add that dimension to your presentation style.

Bottom line? Make sure there isn't anything that looks unprofessional like a kitchen sink piled with dirty dishes in your background.

# THE LIGHTING

I find this is a tricky one to handle. I have wondered around my house and home office trying to find the best lighting. I turned on the camera on my laptop and found that a room with lots of natural light worked best.

One key is that light is best coming from in front of i.e. from behind your screen. A window where the light comes from behind does not work very well. There are also professional lighting options in the marketplace such as ring lights and LED panels. You might also check out inexpensive portable "softbox lighting kits" that come in a bag.

# VIRTUAL PRESENTATION NOTES

Using notes when presenting virtually is always a challenge. This is because the camera is focused directly on your face and eyes. When you look down at your notes it is often distracting.

One thing you can do is to share your screen with your audience along with key points that you are conveying at the same time. This is EXACTLY what I recommend that you do in front of a live audience. In that way, you won't need notes.

There are also apps out there that will allow you to have your notes displayed on your screen and not on your audience's screen.

Another option I used recently where I was producing a presentation for You Tube was to use my iPad as a teleprompter located on a stand right about my laptop screen. My assistant (Ok. My significant other) down the screen on the iPad as I went through my presentation. The iPad was so close to the camera at the top of my laptop screen that it looked like I was looking directly into the camera and therefore the audience. Perfect!

These days there are also affordable portable teleprompters that can be affixed to laptops that can also be used by presenters. These are a great option if you want to read a script and be sure that every word is well thought out ahead of time.

## EYE CONTACT

I see so many different angles these days of people presenting via their laptops that I am of the mind that as long as you are looking directly into the camera just about anything is acceptable. People are used to people looking down into a laptop on their desk, up to a camera on a large screen connected to their desktop, or directly ahead.

There are diverse views on where the eyes should be. Some advocate looking directly into a laptop screen's camera by investing in a tripod. I have simply stacked books up to hold my computer and webcam at eye level!

If you want to see the many ways that people are looking into their webcams these days simply watch a newscast. You will see the newscast professionals in a studio sometimes looking up, down, or at eye level. You will also see the people they are interviewing doing the same.

The glare from glasses is also a challenge that many folks face... including myself. I have tried all kinds of things to counteract this. I am not convinced that any of them reduce the glare completely.

You can try a couple of things. For example, walk around with your smartphone in selfie mode and see where you can best set up without glare from your glasses. You can also try different positions for your lights (portable room lamps) to see where best to locate your laptop.

I have also seen a tip that if you tilt your glasses down a bit it can work. Women can put clips in their hair and rest the arms of their glasses on these. Or you can wear a headset and set your arms under the headset headband in a similar manner. People get used to some glare from glasses and in the end will tend to have it go unnoticed to the point of not being distracted.

# YOUR DELIVERY

There are a lot of skills that come into play whether presenting to an in-person audience or a virtual one. Here are some tips that will help you to deliver with confidence in a virtual scenario:

If you are using slides have a hard copy just in case you have to call in. Same holds true for your notes i.e., have a copy handy.

If you are part of a team make sure that you at least "seem" that you are paying attention when another team member is presenting. Don't fiddle with notes or be looking around on your screen. If you as a team member don't seem interested, it is very distracting.

Have a list of participants and interact with them by name. There is nothing that makes a connection better than to use a person's name.

Don't try to watch any questions or comments that are coming in as your presenting. You WILL get sidetracked. Try to have a colleague keep track and manage this at an appropriate time.

Have a backup plan ready in case of equipment failure. Will you connect everyone on a conference call with a number they can call in on? Will you email everyone with this information or will someone else?

Indicate that you will send them more information via links to blogs etc. after the presentation so that you don't have to drill into detail during the presentation.

Be your natural self and enjoy the time you spend sharing your ideas! Remember, the points for delivering with confidence shared throughout this book still will give you the playbook you need to have a successful delivery.

# CHAPTER 9
# THE CHECKOUT LIST!

The Curtain Lowers...

While reading this book you've had the opportunity to discover many ideas that will put you on the road towards becoming a more confident, eloquent and competent presenter.

You've no doubt come to the realization that there are some very concrete actions that you can take to help you reach your goals as a presenter. Nobody else in the world can give you their confidence. You don't need it! You already have confidence within yourself. Your quest should be to uncover it, acknowledge it, nourish it and allow it to grow. Give yourself a chance to be the best you can be!

In the final pages of this book I've included some quick reference Checklists that you can use to jog your thoughts around some key points for future presentations. I hope you find them useful.

Remember to use the tools and techniques described in this book to assist you in making your presentation a very positive experience for both you and your audience. Have faith in the techniques presented. They work!

I'd like to close by thanking you for letting me share my ideas with you, and from the bottom of my heart wish all the best in your future presentations. I sincerely hope that in some small way I have inspired you. I'd love to be fortunate enough to see you in action some day. Break a leg!

# Index Of Checklists


- **Overcoming Stage Fright**
- **A Post Mortem On Your Delivery**
- **Creative Ideas**
- **Development Steps**
- **Visual Aids**
- **Remedies For Dry Material**
- **Managing Audience Members**

# OVERCOMING STAGE FRIGHT

- Recognize that stage fright is normal.
- Don't over-react to physiological reactions that you may be experiencing. Your audience won't see them anywhere near as much as you exaggerate them in your mind.
- Practice! Practice! Practice!
- Don't "over-read" your audience's body language, they're on your side.
- Use visual aids to guide you. Display one at the very beginning of your presentation to focus the attention away from you.
- Wear something new, it will make you feel special.
- Take a deep breath before you begin and psyche yourself up.
- Use a structure, then you know you're doing things which will make it easy for your audience to follow.
- Recognize that it isn't magic for anyone. It's planning, hard work and determination that lead to success.

# 2. A POST MORTEM ON YOUR DELIVERY

**Did you ...**

- Have enough direct eye contact?
- Speak at an easy-to-listen to tempo?
- Speak loudly enough?
- Smile?
- Have any distracting habits?
- Appear relaxed?
- Gesture freely and naturally?
- Project interest and enthusiasm?
- Allow enough time to cover the subject in enough detail?
- Have your points well organized?
- Make it flow naturally with smooth transitions?
- Describe anything in a light and entertaining way?
- Have a smooth beginning?
- Have a smooth ending?
- Get your message across?

# 3. CREATIVE IDEAS

**Try adding:**

- Demos
- Graphs
- Posters
- Handouts
- PowerPoint
- Music
- Food
- Discussion groups
- Guest speaker(s)
- Interesting facts/trivia
- Creative agenda items
- Shocking statistics
- Quotations
- Real-life stories/examples
- Add color
- Pamphlets
- Rhetorical questions
- Amusing anecdotes

# 4. DEVELOPMENT STEPS

**Remember AMORE...**

- AIM – establish the purpose of your presentation
- MOTIVATION – articulate why your audience should listen to you
- OUTLINE – create an Outline by:
  - Brainstorming ideas
  - Selecting the main ideas
  - Organizing the main ideas
- RECAP – summarize your main ideas
- ENDING – closing words

# 5. VISUAL AIDS

- They shouldn't be too busy, for example, use six points per visual.
- Add illustrations.
- Add graphs.
- Add color.
- Are they legible?
- Do you have titles on each/most visuals?
- Use point form for key words or phrases.
- Is the lettering large enough?
- Have you checked figures for accuracy?
- Are you using a variety of visuals?
- Have you tested equipment ahead of time?

# 6. REMEDIES FOR DRY MATERIAL

- Get your audience participating/discussing your ideas.
- Jazz it up with some snappy visuals such as photographs, video clips, clipart or graphs.
- Use a variety of media.
- Ask rhetorical questions to spark interest, for example: "How do we think this new application will impact your organization?" Then, proceed to answer it.
- Use real-world examples to elaborate on certain points.
- Try to build in a "war story" around some key points.
- Reference something amusing that has happened.
- Put in some shocking statistics.
- Add a quotation from a notable person or newspaper article.

# 7. HANDLING HOSTILE AUDIENCE MEMBERS

- Don't just react and lash back to an emotional statement that someone has made. Count to 10. Seriously, count to 10!
- Do stick to the facts.
- Elaborate on your points to ensure that there's a clear understanding of the facts or your ideas.

Try to understand also where they are coming from.

- Ask the questioner why he/she feels the way they do.
- Ask the rest of your audience if they all feel the same way.
- Acknowledge that there are different points of view and that's AOK.
- Tell your audience you understand why they feel the way they do.
- Stay cool and calm, they are challenging/attacking your ideas, not you!
- Above all...keep to the high road and keep the conversation courteous at all costs

# ABOUT THE AUTHOR

## John Spencer

John Spencer started his career in IT and quickly realized he loved training people. He overcame his own stage fright and became an independent trainer, teaching over 8,000 people the art of presentation techniques in his in-person seminars. Subsequently he held senior management positions in the private sector and sold millions of dollars worth of business. His presentations took him around the world to places as diverse as Buenos Aires, Tokyo, London, and Bern, Switzerland. He's has also created an online course on Win-Win Presentations to share his insights with others. See www.winwinpresentatioins.com

Made in the USA
Columbia, SC
22 May 2021